Praise From Non-fiction Authors On The Merits Of Writing A Book...

"Writing my books is definitely the most important investment I have made in my business. It totally changes people's perception of you, increases your day rate by 100 percent and brings you into contact with people and opportunities that would never normally come your way. I am still amazed by the number of people I meet who know of me already because of the books. They are the only advertising anyone would ever need."

~ Will Murray author of Corporate Denial: Confronting the World's Most Damaging Business Taboo

"It is probably the single most successful thing I did to make me stand out from my competitors."

~ John Ventura, author of Law for Dummies

"Being a published author has provided me with a significant second platform of authority. My business experience and achievements to date are critical for sure but being published has extended that authority beyond the world of project management into a wider audience. As an author I am finding doors opening with greater ease and indeed, in some cases, the doors of opportunity are being opened for me by others – which is a very nice experience, especially if you are 'lazy' like me!"

~ Peter Taylor, author of Lazy Project Manager: How to be twice as productive and still leave the office early

"When I started my business there were quite a few speakers on the subject but I was the only one with a bestselling book in the market and it resulted in a quantum leap in bookings to speak at conferences. I've since written seven more books and each time a new book hits the shelves I receive a boost in business on the speaking circuit."

~ Catherine De Vrye, author of Good Service is Good Business: 7 Simple Strategies for Success

"You're never "too busy" to write a book. It is the most important and valuable form of marketing there is."
~ David Meerman Scott author of Cashing In With Content: How Innovative Marketers Use Digital Information to Turn Browsers Into Buyers

"A book makes you stand out from the crowd when pitching for consultancy work."
~ Annemarie Caracciolo, author of Smart Things to Know About Teams

"A published book (accent on 'published') can bring a string of powerful indirect benefits. It can boost a CV. It can take the place of a business card, with 1000 times the impact. It can open up lucrative speaking or consulting opportunities. It can enhance an author's reputation in a definite target market."
~ Barry J. Gibbons, former CEO of Burger King and author If You Want to Make God Really Laugh Show Him Your Business Plan: 101 Universal Laws of Business

"Publishing a book has allowed me and my business to achieve significant new credibility. The journey from the initial idea through to seeing copies of your book in the hands of customers is exhilarating. The journey required a heightened level of commitment but the prize was worth every ounce of energy. New doors open, your profile and authority are seen in a different light, it becomes easier to turn business enquiries into contracts and other platforms, for you and your business, emerge. Since writing *Turn Your Salesforce into Profit Heroes* I have been on TV and had numerous articles published in respected journals and online for my industry. All that plus the buzz of seeing your work professionally presented on a retailer's shelf or website."
~ Peter Brook, author of Turn Your Sales Force into Profit Heroes: Secrets for unlocking your team's inner strength

"It established me as a guru in my field."
~ Robert W. Bly, author of The White Paper Marketing
Handbook: How to Generate More Leads and Sales with
White Papers, Special Reports, Booklets, and CDs

"Being a published writer has generated consultancy and coaching work for me, not to mention invitations to speak at conferences and run workshops. In many ways, the royalties a book earns are the least important part of the financial equation."
~ John Middleton, author of Writing the New
Economy: The Ultimate E-business Library

"As a consultant it is critical to be credible in front of clients, especially in the early stages of the relationship. One of the ways to develop near instant credibility is to have published books in the area of expertise in which you are consulting. There have been numerous occasions where, because of the books I have written, the client engages more readily and at a different level. This not only helps to build relationships and allow the client to trust your professional judgement, but it also helps to close sales."
~ Andrew Holmes, author of Smart Things
to Know About Risk Management

"Having a book published bestowed instant credibility and authenticity. The result of being a published author is that I am taken more seriously. Since the publication of *The Book of Luck* my network of contacts has broadened considerably and as a consequence I have won search assignments that otherwise I would not have been considered for. I have found that doors have opened that previously would have been closed and I use my book as a calling card to speak to people at the highest level. The book has replaced my company brochure. The publication of a book opens up marketing opportunities second to none. My advice to anyone in a consultancy business is, forget the brochure and produce some original material in a book and you will reap the benefits."
~ Anne Watson, co-author of The Book of Luck - Brilliant Ideas
for Creating Your Own Success and Making Life Go Your Way

"By far the most credible way to build your brand is to get a book published. A published book opens doors, it gets people to pay more attention to you, it adds robustness to your CV, it generates more enquiries, it gives you the best calling card possible as well as cool collateral for meetings and conferences and it starts the process of becoming a thought-leader."

~ *Nicholas Bate, author of Instant MBA: Think, perform and earn like a top business-school graduate*

How to write a book in 33 days

2nd Edition

Establish yourself as an expert, develop your brand, protect your intellectual property, make more money.

Karen McCreadie

Contact Author: karen@wordarchitect.com
Author website: www.wordarchitect.com
Published by: Word Architect Publishing
Cover Design: BookPOD.com.au
Typeset & Internal Design: BookPOD.com.au
Cartoons: Emanuel Pavel (emanuelpavel@gmail.com)

ISBN: 978-0-9561830-1-9 (pbk)
eISBN: 978-0-9561830-2-6 (e-book)

Contents

Introduction...3

PART ONE: THE WHY

Chapter 1: Develop Your Brand 11

What Is Branding? 14

Why Is Brand Development So Important?........................ 15

Differentiate Yourself 15

Establish Relationships.. 17

Makes Business Easier.. 20

Summary of Key Points.. 22

THE BENEFITS 26

Chapter 2: More Sales and Easier Sales.....................31

Generate More Leads.. 32

Close More Sales Without the Struggle 34

Nurture Loyalty and Reactivate Lapsed Clients 38

Summary of Key Points.. 38

Chapter 3: Charge Higher Fees 41

Summary of Key Points.. 44

Chapter 4: Create Additional Revenue Streams 45

Summary of Key Points..48

Chapter 5: Diversify and Expand Your Career........................51

Summary of Key Points..54

Chapter 6: Become a Thought Leader and Protect Your Intellectual Property..57

Summary of Key Points..60

Chapter 7: Is Writing a Book Right for You?........................63

A Word on Timing..67

Summary of Key Points..68

PART TWO: HOW TO WRITE YOUR BOOK

Chapter 8: Sharpen the Axe – Strategy (Days 1 – 2)............73

What Is Your Intention?..74

Know Thyself 76

Putting On Your Marketing Hat 78

Who Is Your Target Market?..79

Not All Clients Are Good Clients..81

What Problem Do You Solve?..82

What Is Your USP?..84

What Benefits Do You Offer? 85

Action Steps..86

Summary of Key Points..87

Chapter 9: Sharpen the Axe Part II – Structure and Substance (Days 3 – 5)..91

Central Premise 92

Title or Working Title..93

Content..95

Step One: Brain Dump..96

Step Two: Order the Idea Clusters..97

Step Three: Create the Table of Contents 98

Structure 100

Book Length 102

Action Steps.. 105

Summary of Key Points.. 105

Chapter 10: Time to Write (Days 6 – 22) 109

The Hallmarks of Powerful Writing 110

    1. Select an Appropriate Voice and Style 112

    2. Be Specific 114

    3. Don't Use Jargon 115

    4. Write as You Speak 115

    5. Make Your Writing Accessible 117

    6. Have Your Research Ready 118

    7. Suspend Your Judgement 118

Additional Ideas to Consider 119

    Carry a Dedicated Notebook.. 119

    Record Your Thoughts 119

    Talk Your Book 120

    Read! 120

Action Steps.. 120

Summary of Key Points.. 121

Chapter 11: From Good to Great (Days 23 – 33) 125

Apply the Polish... 126

    1. Read It Out Loud 126

    2. Review It for Additional Material 127

    3. Acknowledge References 128

    4. Stay Focused on the Objective 131

    5. Step Away From the Book 132

    6. Edit Ruthlessly 132

    7. Get Feedback and Edit Again.. 133

    8. Get It Professionally Edited and Proofread 135

The All-Important Cover.. 138

Action Steps...139

Summary of Key Points...140

Chapter 12: Problems?..143

Help! – I Hate Writing! 143

Help! – Writing Hates Me!...144

Help! – I Can't Find the Time! 145

Summary of Key Points...145

Chapter 13: Hire a Ghostwriter 147

How Does Ghostwriting Work? 149

Advantages of Hiring a Ghostwriter 152

Structure 152

Content 153

Speed 154

Leverage 154

Assessment 155

Contacts 157

Disadvantages of Hiring a Ghostwriter...........................157

Cost 157

Ownership..158

Hiring A Ghostwriter Might Suit You If: 159

Cost of Hiring a Ghostwriter..159

Where Could I Find a Ghostwriter?.................................161

What Will I Need to Do?...163

Manage Expectations 164

Summary of Key Points...166

PART THREE: WHAT ARE THE PUBLISHING OPTIONS?

Chapter 14: The Old Way – Traditional Publishing 173

Advantages of Traditional Publishing 174

Credibility 174

Production..177

Marketing...179
Disadvantages of Traditional Publishing 180
    Hard to Secure...180
    Long Lead Time 181
    Loss of Control 182
    Poor Financial Rewards 183
Who Is Best Suited to Traditional Publishing? 185
Who Are Traditional Publishers Most Interested In?........186
Securing a Traditional Publishing Contract..............187
    Publisher Hierarchy 187
    Preparing a Publishing Proposal 189
Summary of Key Points..193

Chapter 15: The Other Way – Self-Publishing 197
Advantages of Self-Publishing 198
    Total Control...198
    Greater Revenue 201
    Future Potential 201
Disadvantages of Self-Publishing.........................202
    Total Control...202
    Significant Up-Front Costs 202
    Sales 203
Who Is Best Suited to Self-Publishing? 203
Summary of Key Points..204

Chapter 16: The New Way – Print-On-Demand (POD) 207
Advantages of Print-On-Demand 209
    Low Up-Front Costs....................................209
    Flexibility 210
    Access to Sales Channels............................211
    POD Is Environmentally Friendly 211
    Fast and Credible..211
Disadvantages of Print-On-Demand 212
    Lower Profit Margin 212

Possible Contract Issues 212

Reputation Question Marks 213

Who Is Best Suited to Print-On-Demand Publishing? 213

A Passing Word on Vanity Publishing 214

Summary of Key Points...216

Chapter 17: The New Way – E-Books 219

Advantages of E-Books..222

Speed to Market...222

Larger Margins 223

Instant Delivery 224

Powerful Marketing Tool 224

Get Traditional Publishers' Attention 225

Disadvantages of E-Books...225

Less Clout Than a Physical Book..226

E-Book Production Checklist 227

Who Is Best Suited to E-Publishing?.................................227

Summary of Key Points...228

Chapter 18: What's the Right Publishing Strategy?......231

The 7 Fatal Book Writing Flaws 235

Summary of Key Points...238

Conclusion 241

Index...245

About The Author..253

This book is dedicated to Andrew McCreadie.
I still miss him every day.

Introduction

Outside of a dog, a book is man's best friend.
Inside of a dog, it's too dark to read!
~ Groucho Marx

If you ask 100 people to list their dreams and aspirations you would probably find "write a book" features somewhere on that list. According to a survey conducted by The Jenkins Group, 81 percent of American adults want to write a book! Give or take a few million that's about 250 million in the US alone. That number would rise considerably when you include all the other people around the world who fancy themselves as an author.

There are those that would argue that this number will diminish as the relevance of books diminishes in our society. For years now people have been predicting the end of the humble book as we rush to embrace new technology which gives us instant access to all the information we could ever need or want. It was assumed therefore that people would simply stop buying books and instead access the same information through the Internet via a plethora of gadgets and gizmos. At the very least people would certainly stop buying printed books and instead access the knowledge or novel electronically. Certainly, when I wrote the first edition of this book e-books were the new "new thing". Although they had been around for decades they were making their way into the mainstream. As evidence that the physical book was not long for this world the prophets of doom pointed to emerging statistics. In 2011 Amazon reported that for the first time ever electronic books outsold printed books and when the Association of American Publishers (APP) released their sales figures for the same year e-books surpassed print in every trade category. And yet, the number of books being bought and sold is steady. These statistics don't prove that the book is dead or even dying, they merely indicate that consumers are buying and reading their books differently. If anything new technology is breathing a new lease of life into stuffy old publishing whether we choose to read our books the old fashioned way or via a Kindle, Sony Reader, Kobo, Nook or an iPad. Just because the medium is changing, the desire for books is not.

So, if books are not heading for extinction, just evolving into new forms, the big question remains, "Does writing a book really deliver all the benefits millions of aspiring authors believe it will?" It may be true that everyone has at least one book in them but is it really worth the blood, sweat and tears often required for its excavation?

The answer to that question depends very much on what you want to write and why and this book is purely focused on the creation of non-fiction books written by experts in their field.

For many years there has been a growing recognition that perhaps writing a book has advantages that go far beyond potential royalty income. However, much of the evidence was anecdotal and scattered across multiple sources. RainToday.com and Wellesley Hills Group rectified that by conducting a much-needed survey, publishing a report called *The Business Impact of Writing a Book.*

Of the business book authors surveyed, an impressive 96 percent reported that publishing a book did deliver genuine benefit by influencing their business either positively (49 percent) or extremely positively (47 percent). The report also goes on to spell out exactly what those benefits are from authors that have experienced the process – warts and all. We all know surveys can be pretty woolly sometimes and statistics can be made to mean just about anything so let's just clarify some detail...

- 94 percent reported that their book improved their brand.

- 95 percent reported that their book generated more speaking engagements.

- 96 percent reported that their book generated more clients.

- 94 percent reported that their book generated more leads.

- 87 percent reported that their book allowed them to charge higher fees.

- 87 percent reported that their book allowed them to generate a more desirable client base.

- 76 percent reported that their book allowed them to close more deals.

The overwhelming outcome of this research was, "Assuming you have something worthwhile to say in a book, write one!"

As a professional ghostwriter and author since 2000, these findings mirror my own experiences. Time and time again I have witnessed the transformation from practitioner to authority figure simply through the publication of a well written, content-rich book. This instant and automatic elevation in status has always coincided with significant business development and growth.

Let's face it, we are bombarded with marketing and advertising – everyone wants our attention. Everyone wants to sell us something. So how do you stand out from the crowd? How do you effectively differentiate yourself from your competitors? How do you gain visibility and generate confidence without breaking the bank? How do you build trust with increasingly discerning buyers?

Unless you have the marketing and brand-building budget of Coca-Cola then one of the most effective ways to achieve these objectives is to write a great book. Forget brand-building promotions or costly print advertising; forget expensive marketing campaigns that attempt to compete for headspace in a cluttered market. Use your time, money and energy writing a valuable, insightful and informative book that truly adds value to your reader. The happy by-product of doing so is you also position yourself as a thought leader in your industry whilst elevating yourself to the lofty heights of "expert" faster than anything else known to mankind. By adding "author" to your resume, not only will you experience the buzz of seeing your name on the cover of your own book but you will gain credibility with your market and raise yourself and your business above your competitors.

If you work in the world of professional services, if you are or aspire to be a consultant, specialist, CEO, speaker, trainer, health practitioner, entrepreneur or business owner and you want to differentiate your business and services from other people in your field, then write a book.

As an exclusive business card, there is no substitute. As a new business development tool, there is no substitute. If you want to take your career to the next level and significantly increase your income, there is no substitute.

Although it's unclear why writing a book has such power the fact remains being an author impresses people! And this is still true today regardless of technology. In fact, it's probably still as impressive *because* of technology.

The growth of social media now means that anyone can publish their opinion and send it out into the world via a blog, Twitter post or Facebook status update. These tools can be great at fostering and creating a community, making timely offers and staying in touch with customers but they do very little when it comes to establishing credibility.

Value is measured by demand, ability and difficulty to replicate. In other words we ascribe value, worth and credibility to something that lots of people want, when there is ability involved in the delivery of that thing and when that ability is rare. And the fact is that not everyone can write a book. The majority of people can write a letter, essay or article. Anyone with a semi-decent vocabulary can write a blog post if the desire strikes them and surely anyone with a pulse can come up with 140 characters of something and send out a Tweet. But not everyone can write a book.

As human beings we admire things that take time to create and we always will because time can't be cheated. It can't be sped up, bought or sidestepped. As technology and innovation makes instant gratification increasingly instant my prediction is that our admiration for things that are not instant will increase, not decrease. As human beings we always gravitate to exclusivity and we will always value and appreciate what we don't have and what we can't create, own or do ourselves. For example, we admire Olympic Gold medallists because we know that they must have dedicated their lives to that goal and worked harder on their sport than we could even contemplate. We visit ancient buildings and watch stonemasons work their craft with wonder. We want to own Scottish cashmere not a mass-produced supermarket special that will disintegrate after the first wash. We admire manufacturing processes that require specialist skill, hand finishing and lifetimes to perfect. We watch David Attenborough's astonishing nature documentaries, knowing that many of them took years of filming to make. We get a glimpse of the natural world that we could never hope to witness ourselves. We may also watch reality TV but we don't admire it. It may be amusing for a while but it's not impressive. Skill, hard work and longevity create reputations and reputations are solidified in the pages of books. When we are seeking solutions or looking to hire someone we want substance and depth, and books, regardless of the technology for reading and distributing them, will always provide a platform to demonstrate that substance and depth.

We may have embraced new media that allows us to communicate with the world in an instant but we still respect the things that take time like a 25-year-old single malt whiskey or a handcrafted piece of furniture, a painting or a book. And that is unlikely to ever change. In many ways as the world speeds up we will come to appreciate the slow, thoughtful and deliberate even more. As such, books will come to be even more valuable not less.

Being an author opens doors, and that's not going to change. It offers avenues for free publicity and it provides you with an opportunity to extend your reach through events, conferences and speaking engagements. A book is your chance to crystallise your thinking and document your intellectual property so you may cement your position at the top of your field. As an author you are viewed as a specialist and specialists are contacted for comment by media commentators and journalists further securing your position in your industry and amplifying your profile. A well written, content-rich book is the ultimate marketing tool at a fraction of the cost of many of the more traditional marketing activities.

How to Write a Book in 33 Days will explore the benefits of becoming an author – including increased profile, revenue and career opportunities. I will explain how to go from idea to finished manuscript faster than you ever imagined. It doesn't have to be a chore. I will walk you through the process I use to write my own and other people's books. So far I've written over 35, including international bestsellers, and I am frequently commissioned to write for mainstream publishers including John Wiley & Sons so this process works. And for the record, I'm not trained as a writer and have no journalistic or professional writing qualifications. So if I can do it, so can you!

Of course, writing your book is only part of the puzzle so we will also explore all the various publishing options available to you for getting your book to market. Once you understand the advantages and disadvantages of each you will be better placed to decide the correct publishing strategy for you and your business.

My genuine hope is you will actually read this book and that it inspires you to make your dreams of being an author come true. After all, as Thomas Carlyle said, *"The best effect of any book is that it excites the reader to self-activity."*

PART ONE

THE WHY

Writing a book could be the smartest business move you'll ever make but it does require time and effort – even if you end up hiring a ghostwriter. So it's important you go into the task with your eyes wide open. If you are going to finish what you start then you need to be suitably inspired and thoroughly convinced the outcome is worth it.

Part one is dedicated to the reasons why you should write a book and what you can confidently expect to achieve if you do, as validated by independent research. This is important as it will hopefully galvanise your determination to become an author. That way when someone interrupts you with some urgent decision, or calls you in the middle of a brainstorming session, you will be able to resist the temptation to be pulled off your task and make sure your book becomes a reality.

Writing a book is not an ego trip, it's a very specific marketing and brand building strategy that can punch well above its weight in terms of business impact.

Chapter 1

Develop Your Brand

You never get a second chance to
make a first impression.

Whether you are running your business empire from a stylish penthouse suite or surrounded by Lego and stuffed animals in the third bedroom – perception is everything. You have to look the part if you are to succeed in business. I remember writing for a very successful serial entrepreneur who had started his tenth business in his early twenties for $5,000 and sold that business just ten years later for over $100 million. He told the story of how he and his business partner would try to win new business, often well-known, well respected brands. In the early days they didn't have the reputation, contacts or plush offices so they created what they called the "Hollywood Set". They hired new furniture, extra staff and computer monitors and set them up in a vacant office next door to their own less impressive office so they would look bigger and more established than they really were. It worked and they landed the big clients. The business partners knew they could do a great job but needed to be given the chance to prove it. They also knew that perception and first impressions matter and did whatever it took to orchestrate the right first impression. I had another client who did something similar only his team called it the "Disney Pitch".

Whatever you call it, you need to exude confidence so your customers and prospective customers trust you can deliver on your promises. Successful business people don't succeed because they manage to bluff some potential clients to get their start. They succeed because they understand perception and do whatever it takes to positively manage perception so they put themselves into a position where they can demonstrate their ability to deliver. It doesn't matter how good you are until you have an opportunity to demonstrate that to customers.

When you are in communication with a new company, or are deciding whether to buy something, or to choose one professional over another, you are searching for evidence to help you make the "right" choice. That evidence is often gathered without your conscious awareness – and everything matters. From the way the receptionist answers the phone, to the quality of the stationery or the relevance of the website. Everything is delivering a message and creating a perception about their ability to effectively do the job. Everything is either accumulating toward a "Yes" or contributing to a "No".

Carl Jung, the famous Swiss psychiatrist who founded analytical psychology, often talked about perception being reality. He believed that our version of reality was nothing more than our individual perception. In other words, reality is subjective and therefore depends on our own unique interpretations, not on cold hard fact. And this has been corroborated by science as well as ancient spiritual texts.

Consequently perception is either your best friend or your worst enemy. People make decisions about whether to buy from you based on the signs they interpret, whether those signs are accurate or fair is irrelevant. Jung showed us that we assign meaning to situations and events that may have absolutely no basis in fact. For example, if you were looking to hire an interior designer and you noticed a spelling mistake on their homepage, that error alone does not mean that they are not a good interior designer. Interior designers don't need to be great at spelling but they do need to have a level of care and attention to detail and the error demonstrates, whether fairly or not, that those qualities are missing.

Nothing can be left to chance, and the businesses that succeed over the long term are the ones that consciously manage perception through the creation and management of their brand. Brand development has long been viewed as the marketing and advertising domain of global corporations. Certainly, not everyone has the budget of Microsoft or Coca-Cola where they can afford to spend millions just to get their name in front of the mass market. What people forget, however, is that every business is developing a brand whether they are aware of it or not. Every communication your business has with a customer, every advertisement they see, every order they make, every conversation they have is creating that brand. And remember these perceptions and assumptions are occurring one mind at a time. You may not be able to get in front of a million customers through TV advertising or some slick viral email campaign. You may not be able to spend millions on print advertising just to tell people you exist, but if you can find cost-effective ways to get your message across, one customer at a time, that can make a huge difference to revenue – especially if you operate in a high-end environment.

If you consciously take control of your brand and positively manage the perception you create within your market then you can transform your income and career, and writing a book is one of the most powerful ways to achieve this outcome. Becoming an author is a quick, cost-effective way to position yourself in your industry, develop your brand, differentiate yourself from your competitors and create awareness of who you are and what you stand for. Through the pages of your book the reader has an opportunity to build a relationship with you, develop trust in your knowledge and appreciate that you have expertise the reader could benefit from.

Time and again I've worked with clients to help them write a book and as soon as they add "author" to their resume (whether they wrote the book or not) the perception of their expertise in their chosen field has exponentially increased. There is no doubt that the businesses that can positively influence their customers' perception of them through the strategic development and management of their brand are the most successful – and in business, nothing shifts perception like being an author. And that goes for small businesses, sole practitioners and multinational giants alike.

What Is Branding?

A strong brand is just a consistently delivered promise. It is the intangible qualities and personality of your business that lives in the mind of your customer. You may not have sat down and formally thought about who you are, what you stand for and what unique benefits you bring to your customers, but your customers will distil answers to those questions every time they come into contact with you and your business. If you don't consciously manage that interaction, your customers and potential customers will make assumptions on everything, from your trustworthiness to your creativity, based on their own personal experiences and judgements.

Every communication you have with your customers or potential customers through advertising, publicity, word-of-mouth communication, the buying experience, service and delivery, billing and complaints handling is either reinforcing that promise and living up to expectations, or it's not.

One of the most potent aspects of branding is consistency or commitment. Social psychologist Robert Cialdini refers to consistency as one of six basic principles of psychology that influence and direct human behaviour. His brilliant book *Influence: Science and Practice* is the result of extensive experimental studies on the "weapons of influence", together with three years of immersion in the world of compliance professionals – salespeople, fundraisers, advertisers and others. Essentially, Cialdini set out to identify what persuaded people to say "Yes" and commitment or consistency was one of those principles.

We admire people with conviction – even when we don't necessarily share their belief. We respect someone who is willing to take a stand and doesn't change their mind every five minutes.

Writing a book demonstrates commitment. After all, it's hard to change your mind when you've crystallised your thoughts and committed them to paper for the entire world to see. There is something admirable and powerful about that.

So long as you deliver on the promise made in your book, and present a united and consistent front between what you write and what you do, then you will effectively build your brand and people will respond positively to your message.

Why Is Brand Development So Important?

Developing a brand is important because it allows you to consciously manage the perceptions your customers and potential customers have of you and your business. And that has significant implications. A brand allows you to:

- Differentiate Yourself

- Establish Relationships

- Make Business Easier

Differentiate Yourself

Believe one who has proved it. Believe an expert.
~ Virgil

Branding is relevant to a business, for example Dell or Microsoft; a product or service, for example Coca-Cola or FedEx; or an individual. Individual brands can either be personal brands or taken a stage further they can develop into personality brands such as Oprah or George Foreman.

Writing a book is a marketing strategy that is particularly relevant to the creation and development of a personal brand. Once you are an author your customers and potential customers will gain a greater awareness of who you are, what you do best and how you can assist them to achieve their goals. And this is true even if they never buy or read your book. Just being known as an author will elevate the perception other people have of you and your ability and you will be able to bask in the glory of assumed authority and expert status.

Having a well written, content-rich book allows you to positively manage your personal brand and will automatically deliver certain advantages. You will:

- Establish yourself as an expert in your field.

- Increase your profile and enhance your reputation.

- Stand out in a competitive marketplace.

- Increase your influence in business and social circles.

Establishing yourself as an expert taps into another of Cialdini's six basic principles of human behaviour – our innate respect for authority. Whether we like to admit it or not, we listen to people in authority – it's drummed into us from a very young age. We automatically trust experts without any real evidence as to whether that trust is justified.

There is a program on UK TV called *The Real Hustle* that alerts viewers to some of the most popular and successful confidence tricks. The number of times the con involves a fake policeman or security guard is alarming.

In one example, patrons had entered a bar and a man posing as a security guard offered to take their coats and bags for safe keeping as there had been a few thefts in the area. Almost without exception the customers handed over their possessions without a second thought. At the end of the evening they would then ask for their belongings back only to learn there was no security guard in the bar and they had been robbed. Of course the people affected all got their things back but they were stunned by how easily they had parted with their belongings based on nothing more than an assumption of authority and a realistic uniform!

Just think of the authority wielded by the doctor in her crisp white coat. This automatic transference of trust is touted as at least part of the mystery of placebo medicine. The fact that sugar pills and distilled water injections can and do heal some patients is one of the most puzzling phenomena in medicine. The common denominator in placebo cases is that the patient often trusts the doctor implicitly. The unquestionable belief and faith they place in their authority figure seems to play a critical role in bringing about the cure.

Bottom line – we trust people in authority and rarely question the validity of their elevated status. Sometimes in the case of con artists this blind acceptance can be very dangerous. Sometimes in the case of placebo medicine and writing a book this blind acceptance can be extremely beneficial. When you transpose the power of authority into the creation of a personal brand it is easy to see why becoming an author has such clout (think author-ity). As soon as you have written a book on a subject you are perceived as an expert in that subject and that expert status gives you credibility when it comes to winning new business.

Handing over power based on perceived authority is irrational behaviour and we should be very wary of it in all walks of life. However, providing you are genuinely offering something of value and writing from a place of integrity and a desire to help, then writing a book can positively tap into this potent force.

Establish Relationships

> *In order to sell a product or a service, a company must establish a relationship with the consumer. It must build trust and rapport. It must understand the customer's needs, and it must provide a product that delivers the promised benefits.*
> *~ Jay Levinson*

A brand allows you to establish a relationship with your customers. Remember, a brand of any type is held in the mind of your customer; it's not a tangible object. Your brand is an impression, a set of values that your market believes represent your product or business. And, of course, the assumption is that those same values will transfer to the customer once they buy that product.

In effect your brand allows your customer to get to know you or your business and what you stand for so they can establish whether they want to do business with you or not. We can see this play out in the long-running rivalry between Microsoft and Apple: the brand war between these two companies has largely come down to personality. Apple have done a particularly good job of branding themselves as the fun, funky, creative, colourful, vibrant alternative to Microsoft's PC. The PC, probably partly due to the persona of Bill Gates, was pigeonholed as the stiff, pencil-pushing, glasses-wearing, dull, drab, colourless, boring computer geek. Apple has amplified that distinction in everything they do and it has clearly influenced sales. In an attempt to dissolve this imbalance Microsoft spent a massive $300 million on a series of advertisements called "I'm a PC" which first aired in 2008. The primary ad opened with a rather bookish little chap in grey slacks and a scruffy brown jacket saying, "Hello I'm a PC and I've been made into a stereotype." What followed were a multitude of ordinary people from all walks of life who use a PC but didn't fit into the dreary stereotype – a tattooed mummy's boy, clothes designers, a teacher in Africa and a man diving with sharks. Some of the ads also featured celebrities including Eva Longoria and Deepak Chopra.

Sadly for Microsoft the ads didn't do much to change the stereotype. Let's face it, which would you rather be – fun, funky and creative or a boring pencil-pushing geek?

A brand allows us to decide if we like something. If we do, then that business can massively increase sales. People do business with people they like. Life is all about relationships. Liking someone is another important aspect identified by Cialdini. Essentially, we are much more likely to be influenced by someone we like.

The famous trial attorney Clarence Darrow once said, *"The true job of a trial attorney is to get the jury to like their client."* In fact, in most courtroom situations the jury will make an initial evaluation and decision as to the guilt or innocence of the defendant within the first five minutes. All the information after that point will go to substantiate the decision they have already made.

A book offers a unique opportunity, not only for you to develop your personal brand, but also for the reader to get to know you. They can establish whether or not they like you or resonate with your message. The reader can work out your values and what you and your personal brand stand for.

Let your reader get to know you through your book – by doing so you create a connection which can allow a relationship to flourish. I've often had the experience of being introduced as the person that wrote such-and-such a book. If the person I'm being introduced to has read the book, they immediately light up and start talking to me as though they have just met a long lost friend, which is lovely. This type of connection is also extremely beneficial in business.

A brand opens doors to:

New Business

If you treat new customers well and consistently deliver on your brand promise, you create loyal customers.

If you continue to treat loyal customers well and consistently deliver on your brand promise, you create passionate customers.

If you continue to treat your passionate customers well and consistently deliver on your brand promise, you create raving fans who bring in more...

Consistency is the key to successful branding. If you write a brilliant book which entices people to your business and then you fail to deliver on your promise, you've lost. Instead use the book as a stepping-stone to raise the bar in your own organisation. When what is written in your book becomes the quality benchmark in your company and your product or service offer consistently meets or surpasses what is expressed in your book, then everyone wins.

Makes Business Easier

*Thinking is the hardest work there is, which
is the probable reason so few engage in it.*
~ Henry Ford

We all have busy lives and as a result we are all searching for a way to minimise the need for analysis and thought, make the right choice and get into action. One way we achieve this is to tune out all the information that is not relevant at any given time. You will probably have noticed this yourself... most of the year you don't notice the car insurance adverts or you change channels or hit the mute button. Then when your insurance is due, you pay attention. We have become very adept at ignoring information that isn't relevant to us.

The other way to avoid thinking is through the use of thinking shortcuts. It's estimated that the average consumer sees up to 3,000 advertising messages every day. And that is on top of everything else we have to think about on a daily basis. Talk about overload! Our brains are instinctively searching for ways to shortcut thinking, make a choice, and move on.

As human beings, we learn by association. We make sense of the world by filtering the information we receive through our five senses and classifying that data for future use. Whenever we experience something new, we automatically scan the environment to log all the associated facts. Although we are not conscious of this process the hippocampus in our brain is taking note of all the people, places, things, time, location and events that categorise the experience. The future occurrence of two or three of those associated facts could then trigger an automatic or conditioned response. Have you ever exploded over something trivial and been embarrassed and confused about your over-reaction once the red mist has cleared? This is usually the result of some old associative connection you've triggered and you've reacted emotionally before the neo-cortex had a chance to kick in. It is therefore a knee-jerk reaction. Evolutionary psychology also makes reference to this idea as "classification before calculus". It states that in an effort to make sense of changing and uncertain events and circumstances the human brain will classify all experiences instantaneously so that in the future you don't have to consciously calculate whether or not it's something to "think" about or not. Brands allow us to classify choices and shortcut thinking. We can assume they are good, buy it and move on.

You've probably heard of Pavlov's dogs – the famous experiment that showed how quickly and efficiently an automatic response could be conditioned into an Alsatian. At first the dogs were fed. Then they were fed at the same time as they heard a bell ringing. Before long the dogs created a conditioned response whereby they connected the sound of the bell to being fed and would salivate in anticipation of food even when none was forthcoming. The bell became the "shortcut" to salivation and this association happens just as readily in human beings.

Brands act like Pavlov's bell.

Brands shortcut the need to think about what to buy because we are drawn to the brands that we recognise, we don't need to worry about whether we are making the right choice and are often happy to pay extra for that peace of mind. A book can develop your brand and allow would-be customers to be assured of your pedigree.

A book has the effect of creating a conditioned response because the authority created by a book automatically bypasses the usual questions and objections at the early stage of the buying process. And that doesn't occur at a critical mass when your book is sitting on the bookshelf of a million would-be readers – it happens one book at a time. If you have a client or prospective client and you've just finished a pitch, being able to hand over your book or refer to your book has the same effect as a heavily branded product.

If I am in the local supermarket and I'm looking for cola I don't think about which is likely to be the best cola – I wouldn't even consider buying anything other than Coca-Cola or Pepsi. Why? Because they have done such a brilliant job of branding their products that I automatically assume they are better even though they are more expensive and I know what they do to a dirty coin! Handing over your book in a sales meeting does the same thing! You bypass all the questions and go straight to "this is the right choice".

If you were to hire a brand consultant they would explore a number of important areas including name development, logo creation, website and other marketing collateral, advertising, signage and packaging. Depending on who you hire you could spend a small fortune or you could enjoy the benefits of branding for a fraction of the cost of many traditional marketing and branding activities. Remember, 94 percent of the RainToday.com and Wellesley Hills Group study reported that their book improved their brand.

Writing a book is therefore not a self-indulgent expense or ego trip to be considered in retirement but a strategic brand and marketing investment capable of delivering impressive results that last for decades.

Summary of Key Points

- Whether you are running your business empire from a stylish penthouse suite or surrounded by Lego and stuffed animals in the third bedroom – perception is everything.

- When you are in communication with a new company, or are deciding whether to buy something or whether to choose one professional over another, you are searching for evidence to help you make the "right" choice.

- That evidence is often gathered without your conscious awareness – and everything matters. From the way the receptionist answers the phone, to the quality of the stationery or the relevance of the website. Everything is creating a perception about their ability to effectively do the job.

- Nothing can be left to chance and the businesses that succeed over the long term are the ones that consciously manage perception through the creation and management of their brand.

- If you consciously take control of your brand and positively manage the perception you create then you can transform your income and career, and writing a book is one of the most powerful ways to achieve this outcome.

- Becoming an author is a quick, cost-effective way to position yourself in your industry, develop your brand, differentiate yourself from your competitors and create awareness of who you are and what you stand for.

- A strong brand is just a consistently delivered promise. Every interaction with your customers or potential customers is either reinforcing that promise and living up to expectations, or it's not.

- One of the most potent aspects of branding is consistency or commitment. Social psychologist Robert Cialdini refers to consistency as one of six basic principles of psychology that influence and direct human behaviour.

- We admire people with conviction. We respect someone who is willing to take a stand and doesn't change their mind every five minutes.

- Writing a book demonstrates commitment. After all, it's hard to change your mind when you've crystallised your thoughts and committed them to paper for the entire world to see.

- So long as you deliver on the promise made in your book, and present a united and consistent front between what you write and what you do, then you will effectively build your brand and people will respond positively to your message.

- A strong brand allows you to consciously manage the perceptions your customers and potential customers have of you and your business which helps to differentiate your business, establish relationships and make business easier.

- Branding is relevant to a business, product or service, or an individual. Writing a book is a marketing strategy that is particularly relevant to the creation and development of a personal brand.

- Once you are an author your customers and potential customers will gain a greater awareness of who you are, what you do best and how you can assist them to achieve their goals. And this is true even if they never buy or read your book. Just being known as an author will elevate the perception other people have of you and your ability, and you will be able to bask in the glory of assumed authority and expert status.

- Having a well written, content-rich book allows you to positively manage your personal brand and will automatically establish you as an expert in your field, increase your profile and enhance your reputation, help you stand out in a competitive marketplace and increase your influence in business and social circles.

- Establishing yourself as an expert taps into another of Cialdini's six basic principles of human behaviour – our innate respect for authority.

- Bottom line – we trust people in authority and rarely question the validity of their elevated status. Sometimes in the case of con artists this blind acceptance can be very dangerous. Sometimes in the case of placebo medicine and writing a book this blind acceptance can be extremely beneficial.

- When you transpose the power of authority into the creation of a personal brand it is easy to see why becoming an author has such clout (think author-ity). As soon as you have written a book on a subject you are perceived as an expert in that subject and that expert status gives you credibility when it comes to winning new business.

- A brand also allows you to establish a relationship with your customers. It allows your customer to get to know you or your business and what you stand for so they can establish whether they want to do business with you or not.

- People do business with people they like. Life is all about relationships. Liking someone is another important principle identified by Cialdini.

- The creation of a personal brand shortcuts the need to think about what to buy because we are drawn to the brands that we recognise, we don't need to worry about whether we are making the right choice and are often happy to pay extra for that peace of mind. A book can develop your brand and allow would-be customers to be assured of your pedigree.

- A book has the effect of creating a conditioned response because the authority created by a book automatically bypasses the usual questions and objections at the early stage of the buying process.

- If you have a client or prospective client and you've just finished a pitch, being able to hand over your book or refer to your book has the same effect as a heavily branded product.

- If you were to hire a brand consultant they would explore a number of important areas including name development, logo creation, website and other marketing collateral, advertising, signage and packaging. Depending on who you hire you could spend a small fortune or you could enjoy the benefits of branding for a fraction of the cost of many traditional marketing and branding activities.

- Remember, 94 percent of the RainToday.com and Wellesley Hills Group study reported that their book improved their brand.

- Writing a book is therefore not a self-indulgent expense or ego trip to be considered in retirement but a strategic brand and marketing investment capable of delivering impressive results that last for decades.

THE BENEFITS

There are many ways that a book can increase your income but it's probably not in the way you initially imagined.

The Holy Grail of income is, of course, passive income. The allure of making money while you sleep is unquestionable. If we consider how one goes about creating passive income the options are however fairly limited.

You could become a property tycoon and make passive income on the rent of those properties. But if you care to investigate past the hype of buy-to-let you will realise that there is nothing passive about keeping tenants happy! In addition you may indeed make money while you sleep but you won't get much of that if you are mortgaged up to the back teeth and any tremor in the interest rates takes another couple of years off your life!

You could write a Christmas song and collect royalties for decades to come. Can you imagine what Slade has made from "So here it is Merry Christmas" or George Michael from "Last Christmas"?

You could join a network marketing operation but again the chances of success are slim. Anyone who has ever really made it in this arena will probably tell you that most of their friends now avoid them like the plague and that success was anything but passive. Years of serious hard work is required – not to mention the hide of a rhinoceros.

Or you could write a book. At least that's what conventional wisdom says! Images of sandy beaches spring to mind; sun loungers and Piña Coladas here we come. A life of ease as the big fat royalty cheques keep rolling in, long after the last word is written.

Writing a book can do truly amazing things for your career and radically increase your income but let's get one thing crystal clear... If you want to write a book because you are convinced it will sell millions and you have already rehearsed your interview for daytime TV superstardom – then think again. Writing a book for the money you'll make in royalty income is pure folly! Forget *Harry Potter* or *Fifty Shades of Grey* – books of that magnitude happen once in a generation. Or as US marketing expert and entrepreneur Seth Godin states, "*The return on equity and return on time for authors and for publishers is horrendous. If you're doing it for the money, you're going to be disappointed. On the other hand, a book gives you leverage to spread an idea and a brand far and wide. There's a worldview that's quite common that says that people who write books know what they are talking about and that a book confers some sort of authority.*"

And that's the whole point. The *real* value of writing a book does not usually come from royalty income. If you have something worthwhile to say then your book can give you massive leverage in the business world. A book bestows authority to the person credited with writing it and therefore acts as a premium business card. As such it can open doors and generate hundreds of thousands, sometimes millions in additional revenue, making the traditional Holy Grail of royalty income a pleasant surprise rather than a prerequisite for success.

Chip Bell, co-author of *Managing Knock Your Socks Off Service* and participant of the RainToday.com and Wellesley Hill Group study said, "*In reality, the income generated most from a book is through additional work. If you're writing for royalties, you probably shouldn't be writing a business book... If you work it, you can probably make at least ten times as much revenue from sources generated through your book than from the royalties themselves.*"

Publishing a book can be an extremely rewarding journey and *can* generate serious money for your business regardless of the size of your royalty cheques. But if your motive for writing the book is royalty income then you are likely to be extremely disappointed. According to a report in *The Times*, of the 200,000 books available for sale in the UK in 2007 only 10,000 sold more than 3,500 copies. In the same year about 86,000 new titles were published and just over 58,000 of those sold an average of 18 copies. No one is going to get rich selling 18 copies of their book.

Forget about potential royalty income. Instead focus on the *other* ways a book can make you money. Instead of crossing your fingers and hoping for a bestseller, take a more realistic and pragmatic approach to the process so that you ensure your book is a success regardless of the fickle finger of fate. No one really knows what makes a bestseller a bestseller – even those inside the publishing industry. Hoping that you are one of those people is not sound business sense. Creating a book to formalise and develop your brand, increase sales and raise your profile is.

The specific benefits you can confidently expect to achieve from writing a book are detailed in the following five chapters:

Chapter 2: More Sales and Easier Sales

Chapter 3: Charge Higher Fees

Chapter 4: Create Additional Revenue Streams

Chapter 5: Diversify and Expand Your Career

Chapter 6: Become a Thought Leader and Protect Your Intellectual Property

Chapter 2
More Sales and Easier Sales

We are all salesmen every day of our lives.
We are selling our ideas, our plans, our enthusiasms
to those with whom we come in contact.
~ Charles M. Schwab

A book can result in increased business opportunities with new customers who have not heard of you before and provide new selling opportunities with existing or lapsed clients.

In another RainToday.com and Wellesley Hill Group research report, *How Clients Buy: A Benchmark Report on Marketing and Selling Professional Services from the Client Perspective,* buyers of professional services were asked how they went about finding providers. Predictably, the top method of finding providers was referrals. In addition:

- 69 percent of buyers found service providers at presentations, conferences or events.

- 69 percent of buyers already knew about the service provider through brand awareness.

- 62 percent of buyers source their service providers from industry websites, articles or stories.

- 60 percent of buyers sought their service providers from trade magazines or stories.

- 43 percent of buyers looked for their service providers from business books.

It's easy to see, therefore, how being an author can create a virtuous circle that taps into all the methods people use to source professional services. Having a book makes you an instant authority figure that gets you noticed by the media who will be more likely to seek you out for an "expert opinion". This in turn makes you more of an expert and you will find it easier to have articles and papers published in trade press.

This will assist your profile and together with the book will make it easier to get speaking engagements, and the chance of you being asked to present at events and conferences is greatly increased – after all, you're the expert who wrote a book on the subject. As a consequence, what you say and write is more likely to be quoted on industry websites and all of this increases your profile or brand awareness. Put it all together and you can seriously extend your reach and influence more people so you can:

- Generate More Leads

- Generate More Sales Without the Struggle

- Nurture Loyalty and Reactivate Lapsed Clients

Plus you'll probably have a whole lot of fun doing it!

Generate More Leads

Having a book lifts your profile and makes it much easier to get good PR. Often that PR is free because of the book which makes it even better. This means that more people know about you and you have an opportunity to generate more business leads on the back of that recognition.

In the RainToday.com and Wellesley Hill Group research, a conclusive 94 percent of authors reported an improvement in lead generation as a result of the book and 56 percent reported a strong or very strong influence.

Just how much of an impact this could have on you, depends on your business. You need to think about return on investment and work out how many new clients you would need to generate for the project to be worthwhile. A high-end consultancy, for example, may realise that one new client would more than pay for the cost of the book. What would happen to that business if the book led to hundreds of new leads which resulted in 5, 10 or 20 new clients every year? It could revolutionise the business.

Having the book also allows you to gain access to organisations that may have previously been out of reach. Being able to cherry-pick organisations you want to work with and target that organisation with a strong proposal and a copy of your book can lead to easier and more lucrative lead generation programs, with far higher conversion rates than traditional marketing.

As Ford Harding, author of *Rain Making: Attract New Clients No Matter What Your Field* and one of the authors in the book effectiveness study said, *"Publishing books has been very advantageous in networking and meeting new people. If I'm interested in talking to someone and I send them my book, the chances of me getting to meet with them are much greater than if I wasn't an author."*

Bob Urichuck, another author in the study said, *"Books have helped me open up more doors than you can imagine."*

Basically the credibility of the book is sufficiently attention grabbing and unusual that a proposal backed by a book will help to bypass the knee-jerk instinct to delete, bin or ignore the communication. Another helping hand is given by the law of reciprocity, another of Cialdini's principles of influence.

The law of reciprocity is the innate desire to balance the books. If someone gives you a birthday present and you forget to reciprocate you feel bad because the unspoken law has been broken. This need for give-and-take and finding equilibrium between the two is so strong it will actually result in some odd situations. Cialdini tells the story of a university professor who sent Christmas cards to people he didn't know to test how many would respond. To his surprise he was flooded with return cards, the majority of which didn't even inquire about his identity. A card was received, an automatic response kicked in and a reciprocal card was returned. It didn't matter that the card was from a perfect stranger!

Cialdini also points out the power of reciprocity when brought into a "business" context. Prior to the 1970s, the Hare Krishna was a fairly obscure organisation. They attempted to raise funds simply by approaching people in the street and asking for donations. Only orange robes and shaven heads didn't go down too well with a suspicious public. Then the organisation went through radical growth both in funding and numbers of followers and it was all down to reciprocity. Before asking for a donation the "target" was given a "gift" – either a book or magazine or the most cost-effective version of all was a little flower. The receiver of the flower felt an internal compulsion to reciprocate the gift with a donation. Even if they didn't want the flower or tried to return the book they still gave a donation. Fundraising went through the roof.

This principle is used widely in marketing in the form of "free gifts" and product samples. But it also kicks in when you send a potential client your book. Use the book to open doors, generate leads, secure appointments and win new business.

Close More Sales Without the Struggle

If you are serious about writing a book then you need to view the project as a marketing opportunity and apply marketing principles to its creation. I'll talk more fully about this in Chapter 8 but for now this means writing to address two separate objectives. You have to deliver genuine value for your reader while at the same time making the book an extended sales pitch for your business.

If you get this balance wrong and bang on about yourself without offering insight and information, the book will fail. If you don't mention your business at all but offer good, solid information then you will miss a valuable opportunity to cement your position in the market and the book will not deliver on its business development objectives. Get that balance right, however, and your book can make sales a whole lot easier because it goes a long way in silencing the conversation and objections a would-be client would normally have at the start of a buying relationship.

To be successful in business you first have to educate your market about the need for your product or service. Without that recognition of need, any sale is an uphill battle.

You also have to enter the conversation your would-be client is already having in their own head. Namely:

- "I don't have the time for this."

- "I don't have the money for this."

- "I don't believe you and it won't work for me anyway."

I wrote a book for a client, and now dear friend of mine, John Vamos. He is founder and CEO of Business Coaching Systems (BCS) and offers a unique coaching methodology that allows business to systematically achieve and surpass their goals and expectations.

What John has discovered is that business problems are never unique. More often than not they are created organically as the business expands. The systems and strategies start to creak under the pressure of growth and before long inefficiencies and performance challenges emerge.

As a result, the BCS method seeks to unpack the business, re-establish the important parameters and implement systems and procedures that can not only expand with the business but deliver consistent results. The benefits obtained through this process can be extraordinary and BCS enjoys strong referral activity.

John says, "*The three biggest issues that confront a prospect are: WHO are you? WHAT makes you think you can help? WHAT can you do for me? The book overcomes those and saves a lot of time in the invisible stage of credibility establishment.*"

A good book therefore makes selling easier and fast-tracks the buying cycle. It establishes credibility and allays fears before a salesperson is even present. It gives would-be customers the opportunity to develop a relationship with you. They are able to read stories and testimonials of other happy clients that may resonate with them. Using case study examples activates yet another of Cialdini's principles of influence – social proof.

Social proof relates to the fact that when we are unsure what to do or which course of action is the right one, we will instinctively look around at what others are doing to determine acceptable or correct behaviour. You can see this play out in exclusive restaurants where diners are overwhelmed by the cutlery choice and will instinctively look around at the other tables to try to determine what utensil should be used in what order. No one wants to make the wrong choice or look foolish so we use social proof to fast-track that process, eliminate risk, relax and move on.

Again marketers have learned how to tap into this phenomenon by using testimonials. They litter their marketing material with quotes from authority figures or recognisable celebrities or from other satisfied customers from the target market. Testimonials allow us to stop thinking and instead go, "Oh look, if Professor Smarty Pants or him from the TV says it's true then it must be!" or "Oh look, it worked for that person and he's like me so it will work for me too!"

If you ask people if they pay conscious attention to testimonials they would probably deny it. But the evidence strongly suggests otherwise. According to the 2012 version of the popular *Social Media Revolution* YouTube clip 25 percent of search results for the world's top 20 brands are linked to user-generated content and 34 percent of bloggers post opinions about products and brands. What's more, a whopping 78 percent of customers trust peer recommendations whereas only 14 percent trust advertisements. In other words we take social proof very very seriously! We may like to think of ourselves as "different" and "unique". We may like to imagine that we are making a rational decision but more often than not we are influenced by what others are doing because we are innately drawn to the herd – especially when we are in unfamiliar territory

Social proof allows us to feel confident that we've made the right choice and what better endorsement of "right choice" than adhering to the advice of a well-known author? Writing a book with a constant eye on marketing allows you to provide genuine value for the reader while also explaining your proposition in detail. The result is one long testimonial. It offers you a phenomenal opportunity to showcase your business and case study your results. It offers you a medium to disseminate your ideas or methodology so that the reader can see themselves in the pages and be assured that you are the right person to help them.

Having a book is also a useful tool for your salespeople as it gives them and their company credibility that competitors may not have. It is especially useful for the less vocal and extroverted salespeople in your team who can use the book to their advantage. Plus if you hate promoting yourself but realise it's an essential part of business, then a book can be a great solution.

Your book will do some of the selling for you by building trust and allowing you or your sales professionals to shorten the buying cycle. Your prospects may not always read it straight away but they will never throw it out. Ford Harding, one of the authors in the book effectiveness study said, *"Several of our clients were people I sent the book to. It sat on their shelf for a while, but when a need within the company arose, they recalled who we were and called us for help."*

Harding goes on to say, *"The book differentiates us from our competition and helps us get big-name client work. Clearly it's been worth it to me, not for the royalties, but for the huge effect it's had on my business. When somebody calls you and says, 'I've read your book and I'd like to hire you,' you know it was worth everything it took to do."*

When prospective customers start calling you then the selling process is made a whole lot easier. You start the conversation at a more advanced level because the book has taken care of the invisible yet vital credibility establishment phase. Your book therefore acts as a vital sales tool to shorten the buying cycle and remove buyer remorse, especially on "high ticket" items.

Nurture Loyalty and Reactivate Lapsed Clients

A book that improves your brand will do wonders to strengthen your existing customer relationships. Invite key clients to your book launch and include the best ones as case studies and examples. Not only do you illustrate how you have assisted others but you can also give your best clients a plug and make them feel special. It's not a sycophantic free-for-all, but done with integrity it can be a win/win for everyone.

Clients that are already working with you can feel comforted that you have published a book. In addition you can use the book as a great reason to go back to lapsed or past customers and reactivate them. The publication of your book offers an excellent opportunity to build loyalty and reach out to people you've lost touch with.

Mark Satterfield, author of *Power Prospecting* and one of the business impact survey participants said, "*It was a great excuse to stay in touch when I interviewed current clients as part of the research for my book. Publishing helped bring my practice into clearer focus.*"

In short your book allows you to differentiate yourself from the competition. You may not be the only person who has written a book in your field but if you can finish your presentation or new business pitch by handing over your published book you will always stand out from those who don't. It's a powerful differentiation tool that can get your foot in the door and edge out your rivals in a competitive situation.

Summary of Key Points

- A book can result in increased business opportunities with new customers who have not heard of you before and provide new selling opportunities with existing or lapsed clients.

- Being an author can create a virtuous circle that taps into all the methods people use to source professional services resulting in more leads, more sales and an opportunity to nurture loyalty and reactivate lapsed clients.

- Having a book lifts your profile and makes it much easier to get good PR. This means that more people know about you and you have an opportunity to generate more business leads on the back of that recognition.

- You need to think about return on investment and work out how many new clients you would need to generate for the project to be worthwhile. A high-end consultancy, for example, may realise that just one new client would more than pay for the cost of the book.

- The credibility of a book is sufficiently attention grabbing and unusual that a proposal backed by a book will help to bypass the knee-jerk instinct to delete, bin or ignore the communication.

- Another helping hand is given by the law of reciprocity, another of Cialdini's principles of influence. The law of reciprocity is the innate desire to balance the books and it is activated when you send a potential client your book. Use the book to open doors, generate leads, secure appointments and win new business.

- If you are serious about writing a book then you need to view the project as a marketing opportunity and apply marketing principles to its creation. You have to deliver genuine value for your reader while at the same time making the book an extended sales pitch for your business.

- To be successful in business you first have to educate your market about the need for your product or service. Without that recognition of need, any sale is an uphill battle.

- You also have to enter the conversation your would-be client is already having in their own head. Namely, "I don't have the time for this", "I don't have the money for this" or "I don't believe you and it won't work for me anyway".

- A good book therefore makes selling easier and fast-tracks the buying cycle. It establishes credibility and allays fears before a salesperson is even present. It gives would-be customers the opportunity to develop a relationship with you. They are able to read stories and testimonials of other happy clients that may resonate with them.

- Using case study examples activates yet another of Cialdini's principles of influence – social proof. Social proof relates to the fact that when we are unsure what to do we will instinctively look around at what others are doing to determine acceptable or correct behaviour.

- Writing a book with a constant eye on marketing allows you to provide genuine value for the reader while also explaining your proposition in detail. The result is one long testimonial. It offers you a phenomenal opportunity to showcase your business and case study your results.

- A book that improves your brand will also do wonders to strengthen your existing customer relationships.

- Clients that are already working with you can feel comforted that you have published a book. In addition you can use the book as a great reason to go back to lapsed or past customers and reactivate them. The publication of your book offers an excellent opportunity to build loyalty and reach out to people you've lost touch with.

- In short your book allows you to differentiate yourself from the competition. You may not be the only person who has written a book in your field but if you can finish your presentation or new business pitch by handing over your published book you will always stand out from those who don't. It's a powerful differentiation tool that can get your foot in the door and edge out your rivals in a competitive situation.

Chapter 3
Charge Higher Fees

One man is as good as another
until he has written a book.
~ Benjamin Jowett

The RainToday.com and Wellesley Hill Group research stated that 87 percent of respondents experienced an increased ability to raise their fees with 53 percent reporting a "strong" or "very strong" influence on their ability to charge higher fees. Author of *Million Dollar Consulting*, Alan Weiss, specifically said, *"You get on the inside track to revenues from the status of being an author and having that credibility. The recognition is huge."*

Weiss goes on to say, *"In terms of business a book is a gold-plated marketing technique; the only thing better is one buyer saying to another buyer 'Hire Alan Weiss.'"*

Being able to charge higher fees comes down to perception and simple economics. If you have a book there is an automatic assumption of ability that only you can screw up. If I am looking for advice on how to buy properties in Wales it's very likely that I would look for someone with that sort of experience and if that person had also written a book called "How to successfully buy property in Wales" then I would view that, rightly or wrongly, as good evidence that I'd found the right person. I would also be prepared to pay extra for that expertise. The book pre-approves his ability and sanctions, or at least justifies, higher fees.

Bob Urichuck, author of *Online for Life: The 12 Disciplines for Living Your Dreams* and participant in the study said, *"It had an immediate impact – it brought me to a higher level of perceived expertise. Now I've got a book, so 1) I'm an authority 2) it's allowed me to charge higher fees and 3) it's given me great word of mouth because that book becomes the best marketing tool you could have."*

As discussed, having a book is the perfect vehicle to create your personal brand. It instantly elevates you to the lofty heights of expert and the experts in every profession from dentists on Harley Street to designers like Prada and Louis Vuitton charge considerably more for their products and services than the rest of the market. There is a premium to be made when you can lift yourself above the crowd.

Those that are considered experts also benefit from Cialdini's final principle that influences human behaviour – scarcity. The principle of scarcity refers to the fact that opportunities seem more valuable to us when they are less available. Marketers use this all the time with limited offers and special editions! The idea that there is only a limited number or a limited time to take advantage of an opportunity is innately motivating for us.

Consumers are suckers for scarcity! Whether it's through limited seats at a seminar, limited editions of porcelain Elvis dolls or Harley Davidson toilet seats, scarcity taps into an innate desire not to miss out – even if what you are missing out on isn't something you'd normally want!

So how does this relate to writing a book? There are millions of books in publication so it's hard to think of them as scarce but when you consider those millions in relation to the entire population – being an author is scarce. That scarcity gives you kudos. It also offers an element of "celebrity" that activates if you are in front of an audience. Just go to a seminar and watch how people rush to the back of the room when the speaker tells the audience he's only got 50 books available today. Of course, he's actually got a trailer load but the participants don't know that.

Scarcity also talks of the exclusivity that comes with being an author. If, for example, you run a management consulting firm and you write a book, you will be the consultant the clients want. People assign more value to opportunities that are less available. Your time is finite so if you have positioned yourself as an expert through your book, people will pay a premium to have access to you.

It's basic economics. You only have so much time in the day so if demand for your services increases because of your book then you can either increase your fees to whittle down demand or you can pick and choose who you supply. You have the opportunity therefore to create a more desirable client base AND make more money from that client base.

For example, it's not possible for me to write all the books I'm asked to write in a year so instead I choose clients that:

- I like or respect.

- Are committed to writing a book and recognise that they will still have to contribute even if they do hire a ghostwriter.

- Recognise their limitations regarding writing and are willing to pay for the expertise.

- Have integrity and want to add to knowledge instead of plagiarising or repackaging existing knowledge.

- Have something genuinely worthwhile to say.

- Want to write a book on a topic that interests me.

I choose to write a handful of books for other people every year. I do it because I genuinely enjoy helping people achieve their dream of being an author. Often the people I work with are busy running successful businesses and finding the time to write a book is virtually impossible. As a result "write my bestseller" stays on their New Year's resolution list to haunt them for years. By hiring a ghostwriter they finally get to cross it off their "To Do" list without the additional workload or stress. And this is especially rewarding when they realise that the book is still *their* book, it's still their ideas represented on the page.

I don't take every job that comes along and I don't have to waste time with tyre-kickers and neither should you!

By the way, a book is of no use to you if you aren't very good at what you do. People are not stupid so they may buy the book but they would never think to engage you in work or ask for advice if that book isn't very informative or useful. A good book only helps you to get to "Yes" so you can demonstrate your ability and go on to surprise and delight your customers.

Summary of Key Points

- The RainToday.com and Wellesley Hill Group research stated that 87 percent of respondents experienced an increased ability to raise their fees.

- Experts in every profession from dentists on Harley Street to designers like Prada and Louis Vuitton charge considerably more for their products and services than the rest of the market. There is a premium to be made when you can lift yourself above the crowd.

- Those that are considered experts also benefit from Cialdini's final principle that influences human behaviour – scarcity. The principle of scarcity refers to the fact that opportunities seem more valuable to us when they are less available.

- Your time is finite so if you have positioned yourself as an expert through your book, people will pay a premium to have access to you.

- You only have so much time in the day so if demand for your services increases because of your book then you can either increase your fees to whittle down demand or you can pick and choose who you supply. You have the opportunity therefore to create a more desirable client base AND make more money from that client base.

Chapter 4

Create Additional Revenue Streams

*The best way to become acquainted with
a subject is to write a book about it.*
~ Benjamin Disraeli

Writing a book forces you to clarify your thinking and hone your intellectual property. It is said that good writing is simply clear thinking made visible. When you sit down to write a book the process will demand a level of contemplation that you may not expect. Luckily there are significant advantages to this deep, extended thought because it often throws up new ideas or product development opportunities. Many times the author will realise just how much they know about their field. That awareness can lead to all sorts of revelations and possibilities about new products and services that the business could offer.

So long as your book is good and readers enjoy it and feel they have benefited from your expertise and advice, then there is a very good chance they will want to hear what else you have to say. Use the book to offer your readers something else of value and direct them to your website so you can up-sell or cross-sell. Offer readers a discount on other products or services or make reference to other aspects of your business offering to pique their interest. You can also use the book to encourage the reader to join your community either through opt-in online communication or by directing them to your Facebook page or encourage them to follow you on Twitter.

Information and access is already seen as the new currency in business. Building a database and creating a community is one of the most important things any business can do for long-term sustainability and growth. Offering something of genuine value through your book can therefore allow you to further penetrate your market as customers or potential customers come to know and recognise you as an important information source. People who buy your book or talk about your book are obviously warm prospects for your business offering or additional information based products.

If your business is content-rich then you can use your book to generate interest and create e-books or special reports to target niche areas within your business. I have worked with a number of clients who fall into this category.

For example, I worked with Paul Burgess on his book *Natural Born Success – Discover the Instinctive Drives™ that make you tick!* Paul had developed a proprietary profiling system called Instinctive Drive (I.D.), which had been independently validated by academic research. The I.D. System™ is one of the few psychometric profiling tools that delve beneath people's behaviour and personality to explore their innate instinct. For example, I *can* work in an organisation, I've done it before many times but after a while I become very restless and pretty miserable. I much prefer the freedom and flexibility of self-employment. I have friends who love the corporate life and can think of nothing more isolating or dull than working alone. We are all different and what makes us tick is very different. As responsible adults we can all make ourselves do things we don't want to do but these things shouldn't be permanent. If you hate your job, for example, and you constantly have to force yourself to do it then you make life needlessly difficult. If you don't understand your Instinctive Drive and constantly go against your own basic nature then everything is a struggle. The I.D. System™ allows you to uncover your instinctive drives or basic nature so you can take steps to become more "in stride" with your innate nature instead of fighting against it. As CEO and founder of Link Up International Paul and his team help people understand themselves and other people better so as to live healthier, happier and more productive lives.

The insights offered by the I.D. System™ have endless applications for professional and personal life. Consequently when we wrote the book we could easily have written something to rival *War and Peace* because of the depth and breadth of the content. In the end we chose to cover the universally relevant topics – career selection, career development, personal relationships, parenting children, health and wealth creation. The book therefore introduces I.D. and illustrates how it plays out in all the important areas of life.

All of the business related material, such as time management, leadership, tackling procrastination and decision-making, did not therefore belong in the introductory book. Adding the business related information would have interrupted the flow and alienated some readers. It is this type of additional material that is therefore perfect for e-books, special reports or member only access on websites. These additional products or services can then be directed toward specific segments of the market, add greater value to that segment and generate additional revenue for the business.

Many of the business people I write for fall into this content-rich category. This is especially relevant for training companies, consultants, coaches, professional services practitioners, and health practitioners who are always developing new material either through new insights or successful case study material. With all this valuable additional content you have several options. You could turn it into additional information products which are sold to your audience as e-books or special reports. Alternatively you could create a members only section of your website to foster greater loyalty and provide additional relevant information to your audience. Or you can distribute this new content via some of the new social media platforms to keep your customers involved and connected to your business. Either option will increase revenue either directly or indirectly.

Frank Bettger, the author of a classic little sales book called *How I Raised Myself from Failure to Success in Selling,* published in 1947, said the quickest way to get what *you* want is to find out what *other people* want and help them get it. Being able to help your clients get what they want while at the same time creating additional revenue is a win/win situation.

If you have a content-rich business you have an opportunity to package that knowledge into products. Those products can be used to create additional revenue or given away as value-add products to strengthen the customer relationships and develop brand loyalty.

Use the book to drive people to your website and collect their email addresses. Pull them toward your social media platforms and use the new content to stay in constant contact with your audience and further establish yourself as an innovator and thought leader in your field. Whatever you do, make sure it's customer-focused and be sure to adhere to privacy law and regulation.

Summary of Key Points

- Writing a book forces you to clarify your thinking and hone your intellectual property. It is said that good writing is simply clear thinking made visible.

- Luckily there are significant advantages to this deep, extended thought because it often throws up new ideas or product development opportunities.

- Use the book to offer your readers something else of value and direct them to your website so you can up-sell or cross-sell.

- Offer readers a discount on other products or services or make reference to other aspects of your business offering to pique their interest.

- You can also use the book to encourage the reader to join your community either through opt-in online communication or by directing them to your Facebook page or encourage them to follow you on Twitter.

- Information and access is already seen as the new currency in business. Building a database and creating a community is one of the most important things any business can do for long-term sustainability and growth.

- If your business is content-rich then you can use your book to generate interest and create e-books or special reports to target niche areas within your business.

- This is especially relevant for training companies, consultants, coaches, professional services practitioners, and health practitioners who are always developing new material either through new insights or successful case study material.

- If you have a content-rich business you have an opportunity to package that knowledge into products. Those products can be used to create additional revenue or given away as value-add products to strengthen the customer relationships and develop brand loyalty.

- Use the book to drive people to your website and collect their email addresses. Pull them toward your social media platforms and use the new content to stay in constant contact with your audience and further establish yourself as an innovator and thought leader in your field.

Chapter 5
Diversify and Expand Your Career

Great is our admiration of the orator who
speaks with fluency and discretion.
~ Cicero

Being an author can take your career in all manner of new directions. Alan Weiss, author of *Million Dollar Consulting* and one of the authors featured in the RainToday.com and Wellesley Hill Group study said, "*It created an entire second career for me, which was consulting to consulting firms and consultants. And that has substantially changed my life and my work ... [writing a book] is one of the two or three most important things I have ever done to market myself.*"

Another author, Jonathon Kranz, who wrote *Writing Copy for Dummies* said, "*It's opened up a whole new aspect of my business that I hadn't explored before, other than the traditional copywriting that I do: I'm now selling training. I started in-house corporate training, and with the authority of the book, that's a real door opener. It's opened up a whole new revenue stream and an avenue for my business that hadn't existed before.*"

For others it takes them into the lucrative world of seminars and speaking. If you want to tread the boards then a book is an essential tool. Not only does it give you credibility but it also gives you a "back of room" sales opportunity. Seminars don't always make money on ticket sales – most of their revenue is created at the end of the seminar when excited participants rush to the back of the room to buy whatever goodies the speaker has for sale. Having attended many seminars I have witnessed this first hand – both as the person selling product and the person waving her credit card around!

Over the years, many of my clients have been speakers. The first book I ever worked on was *SalesDogs* by Blair Singer. At the time I had left my last fulltime position as the manager of a personal development program in Sydney, Australia and had started out on my own as a marketing consultant. A client of mine mentioned that a friend of his was looking for a writer to rewrite his manuscript. That friend was Blair Singer. I had never done this type of work before but I wanted to move into writing so Blair and I spoke on the phone. I suggested that I write a few initial chapters without a fee and if he liked the book we would continue and he would pay me and if not then he could continue his search for a writer. I rewrote it and added additional content and the book went on to be published by Warner Business Books as part of the Robert Kiyosaki's *Rich Dad's Advisors* series. It is now an international bestseller and Blair has rebranded his entire business around the theme of *SalesDogs*.

Often by their own admission, really good speakers are not necessarily really good writers. The communication style is, of course, different and requires different skills. You can say things on stage that you simply can't say in a book. For example, a speaker might talk about a study that illustrates some fact or other and no one in the audience thinks to question it. In truth, they probably won't even remember it, but if you say the same thing in a book it sounds weak and meaningless. The reader wants to know what study it was and who conducted it – writing requires precision and accuracy that speaking sometimes doesn't.

A presenter's main revenue rarely comes from ticket sales but through the product he or she has the opportunity to sell to a highly motivated audience. So long as they deliver value on stage and the audience likes what they hear then there is a very good chance that the speaker will sell books, DVD training programs or additional seminars. Having a book is an essential part of that repertoire.

I wrote a book for an Australia based stock market trader and teacher who is very well known as someone who teaches people how to invest in the stock market without the hype and nonsense. In his evolution as a trader he made just about every mistake possible and consequently he is a brilliant teacher and enjoys an outstanding reputation. As a result he has been asked to speak all over the world, often in front of thousands of people. Every time I see him he kicks himself, "If only I'd had that book I'd have sold thousands of copies by now!"

The book was 95 percent finished and I even had John Wiley & Sons very interested in publishing it! But it never did reach the finishing post because competing demands for his time always won out over finishing the book. I lost count of the times I was asked by publishers, bookshops and potential readers if that book was finished but it never did make it to the shelves. As a result my client missed out on a great opportunity to extend his reach and increase his profile and revenue. But perhaps more importantly, readers missed out on learning from his extensive knowledge and often painful experience. We don't always need to make our own mistakes in life and losing money the hard way is one that you can just as easily learn from someone else.

> *Employ your time in improving yourself by*
> *other men's writings so that you shall come*
> *easily by what others have laboured hard for.*
> *~ Socrates*

Speaking engagements can offer a very lucrative diversification to your business. Nassim Nicholas Taleb, a former quantitative analyst and derivatives trader who made US$40 million shorting the market on Black Monday in 1987, is now Dean's Professor in the Sciences of Uncertainty at the University of Massachusetts. Taleb is also often described as one of the most sought-after thinkers in the world, thanks to his books *The Black Swan* and *Fooled by Randomness*, and charges up to £35,000 (US/AU$50,000+) for lectures. That reputation was not forged from the fires of the 1987 stock market crash but through the pages of his books. He was able to formalise his intellectual capital by writing books on probability that have put him firmly on the world stage. Of course, he would have been known inside the financial world but it was his books that gave him the global recognition he now enjoys.

Even if you don't want to do the rounds as a speaker in anything more than a part-time basis, having a book will allow you to pick and choose engagements. It's also worth noting that if you do have speaking engagements and already have access to a "natural market", in other words if you have access to people that are very likely to buy your product, then traditional publishers will look very favourably on you. But we'll cover more on that in Chapter 14.

Writing a book for the express purpose of creating a business development tool means that the success of the book is no longer down to the number of units sold. The true value is delivered not through royalty income but through an increase in business activity, better clients, and better relationships with existing clients, better leads, more opportunities to generate income and more opportunities to diversify your business. In short, writing a book can lead to more kudos, more money, more opportunity and probably more fun!

Summary of Key Points

- Being an author can take your career in all manner of new directions including consultancy, training, seminar and speaking opportunities.

- If you want to tread the boards then a book is an essential tool. Not only does it give you credibility but it also gives you a "back of room" sales opportunity.

- A presenter's main revenue rarely comes from ticket sales but through the product he or she has the opportunity to sell to a highly motivated audience.

- Having a book is an essential part of that repertoire.

- Speaking engagements can offer a very lucrative diversification to your business.

- Even if you don't want to do the rounds as a speaker in anything more than a part-time basis, having a book will allow you to pick and choose engagements.

- Writing a book for the express purpose of creating a business development tool means that the success of the book is no longer down to the number of units sold.

- In short, writing a book can lead to more kudos, more money, more opportunity and probably more fun!

Chapter 6

Become a Thought Leader and Protect Your Intellectual Property

Writing crystallizes thought and
thought produces action.
~ Paul J. Meyer

Your intellectual property (IP) is an extremely valuable asset in your business. Whether you have proprietary ideas or techniques or simply years of successful business experience and plenty of happy clients then you need to find a way to tell the world about it. And there is no better way than a book.

Writing a book not only formalises your thinking but it can establish and protect first mover advantage. In other words, if you have something valuable to say you should say it before someone else steals your thunder. Many a famous discovery has been pipped at the post by a more vocal competitor!

Augustin Le Prince was the first to develop a working prototype of a motion picture camera but he wanted to perfect it. In the meantime, Thomas Edison formalised his similar invention with a patent. So Edison, not Le Prince, is known as the father of the motion picture camera – despite Le Prince's version being far superior.

Even the legendary Charles Darwin was almost beaten to the evolutionary punch. He had documented his findings from his voyage on the *Beagle* but had never quite got around to publishing them. Instead he put his musings away, fathered ten children and devoted himself to the study of barnacles for eight years!

According to Bill Bryson in his brilliant book *A Short History of Nearly Everything*, Darwin's own manuscript might have remained locked away until his death had it not been for a letter arriving from a young naturalist named Alfred Russel Wallace which outlined his own theory of evolution. Darwin even reflected, *"If Wallace had my manuscript sketch written out in 1842, he could not have made a better short abstract."*

In the end Wallace and Darwin's ideas were presented together and Wallace was very amenable to the idea as he accepted his ideas came in a flash of inspiration as opposed to years of study and hard work. As a result Darwin is the undisputed father of evolution – but it could have been very different had it not been for a tip-off letter from a distant admirer.

If you have something to say – you need to say it and you need to say it now. Before someone else beats you to it! There can be few things worse than being tortured by a book that you feel you should write (believe me I know!). But waking up one morning to realise that someone else has written *your* book must surely be worse still – especially if it goes on to be a huge success! In fact, a Scottish gardener called Patrick Matthew had come up with the idea of natural selection more than 20 years before Darwin or Wallace, but very few people knew about it.

If you genuinely feel that your business offers something unique and different then you'd better say it – before someone else does. And there is nothing like the process of writing a book to establish if you are correct or not.

Writing a book, even if you hire a ghostwriter, forces you to think about your ideas or methodology in a way that you probably have not done in the past. I can't emphasise this point strongly enough and one client springs to mind that illustrates the point perfectly. There was no doubt he knew his methodology, he'd created it and he had created a successful consulting business around the methodology. He wanted a book and hired me to write it for him. As the project progressed, however, it became increasingly obvious that whilst he knew the methodology inside out he'd never had to explain it as a cohesive whole. The methodology itself had evolved over time, each new piece just tacked on to the last. In a consultative setting this didn't pose a problem because questions could easily be answered in normal conversation. This interaction is not possible in a book and so the author must be extremely clear and precise about what they wish to convey.

Every time I would meet this client to gather content and interview him on his methodology he would explain it in a new way. He used an acronym to describe the various elements of his process but the acronym did not actually reflect the order or syntax of the process. Within that process he was still deciding what to call one of the sections ten months into the project. Again this didn't matter in a consulting situation but it absolutely matters in a book.

If your reader doesn't understand something or it doesn't make sense, or there are holes in the argument or flaws in the thinking, then the reader will switch off and close the book. The reader can't ask the author for clarification – it has to be crystal clear from the start. What I came to realise is that he had never engaged in the depth of thinking required to write a book; it became untenable and I pulled out of the project.

Writing a book really does force you to think. Remember, good writing is clear thinking made visible. If you have not engaged in clear thinking then the book will reflect that and you will not achieve your goal. If however you appreciate the importance of clarity, logical arguments and proper structure then there really are few better ways to crystallise your intellectual property. A different client who I've written two books for has gone so far as to say that writing his books were the *only* way he genuinely created new IP.

And remember, not every book is unique. There are millions of books on sale, for example, and yet some stand out because they have found a unique way to express their ideas using a clever "hook". My first book, *SalesDogs*, assigned a breed of dog to different sales personalities – the idea being that you could be a Basset Hound, Golden Retriever, Chihuahua or a Poodle and still succeed in sales. You don't need to be the stereotypical Pit Bull! Often people wrestle with the idea of writing a book because their topic is not unique or it is not going to change the world, but few books do. Write a good book, that you are proud of, that showcases your business credentials, and helps you and your readers reach their goals.

Positioning yourself as a thought leader is essential if you are to increase business and have clients come to you. A book is a brilliant way to galvanise your position in your field and drive business to your door. And as one author from the book effectiveness report said, "*It pushed me to deepen and expand my intellectual capital.*"

There is nothing that will sharpen your appreciation of your offer, what you do, what strengths and opportunities you bring and how you can genuinely help your clients than writing a book. You may be pleasantly surprised to realise just how much you know and how useful that knowledge is to others.

Summary of Key Points

- Your intellectual property (IP) is an extremely valuable asset in your business. Whether you have proprietary ideas or techniques, or simply years of successful business experience and plenty of happy clients, then you need to find a way to tell the world about it. And there is no better way than a book.

- Writing a book not only formalises your thinking but it can establish and protect first mover advantage. In other words, if you have something valuable to say you should say it before someone else does and steals your thunder. Many a famous discovery has been pipped at the post by a more vocal competitor!

- There can be few things worse than being tortured by a book that you feel you should write (believe me I know!). But waking up one morning to realise that someone else has written *your* book must surely be worse still – especially if it goes on to be a huge success!

- Writing a book, even if you hire a ghostwriter, forces you to think about your ideas or methodology in a way that you probably have not done in the past.

- The reader can't ask the author for clarification – it has to be crystal clear from the start.

- If you appreciate the importance of clarity, logical arguments and proper structure then there really are few better ways to crystallise and protect your intellectual property.

- Often people wrestle with the idea of writing a book because their topic is not unique or it is not going to change the world, but few books do. Write a good book, that you are proud of, that showcases your business credentials, and helps you and your readers reach their goals.

- Positioning yourself as a thought leader is essential if you are to increase business and have clients come to you. A book is a brilliant way to galvanise your position in your field and drive business to your door.

- There is nothing that will sharpen your appreciation of your offer, what you do, what strengths and opportunities you bring and how you can genuinely help your clients than writing a book.

Chapter 7

Is Writing a Book Right for You?

I can't write a book commensurate with
Shakespeare, but I can write a book by me.
~ Sir Walter Raleigh

It all sounds fabulous doesn't it! More sales, easier sales, new revenue streams, better clients, career development opportunities and credibility by the bucketload! There is overwhelming evidence and validating research that writing a book is a very shrewd business move.

But, is it the right marketing strategy for you? Should you invest the time and/or money to write your book or should you redirect those finite resources elsewhere?

In order to find out which is more suitable to you and your situation, you need to answer a few other questions:

1. Would it be beneficial to you to create a personal brand, become a recognised expert in your field and therefore differentiate yourself from your competitors? If so, then a book can make a positive difference.

2. Is what you are promoting high value, lower volume? A book is most effective when the "ticket price" is higher but the volume of sales is lower.

3. Is your business based on creating strong customer relationships and building loyalty? If it is, then writing a book can nurture that process.

4. Is your field competitive? If it is, then having a book can be a brilliant way to stand out from your business rivals.

5. Is your business content-rich? If it is, then you will find writing the book much easier and that content will also allow you to develop additional information based products.

6. Do you want to expand your business or take your career in new directions, such as speaking or consulting? If you do, then a book can be a powerful accelerator toward that goal.

7. Are you starting a business, rebranding a business, or have you recently merged and want to reposition the new business? If so, then a book can be an excellent cost-effective springboard to free publicity, more business and improved brand awareness.

Being good enough is no longer good enough. You could have the best product or service in your category anywhere in the world but unless you can effectively let people know about it, then it doesn't really matter. You will never get the opportunity to sell that product or service or demonstrate your talent, skill or ability in your field. That's why sales will always be the engine of any business and that's why very good salespeople are paid the big bucks. Unless you can reach your market then ability, skill and product ingenuity lie dormant.

The Internet has revolutionised the way business works and we frequently hear of the opportunity that this brings but it is not all peaches and cream. Depending on your business, you may not just be competing with similar businesses in your geographic location but with the entire global marketplace. As a writer, for example, I am no longer competing with other writers in my local area; I'm competing with writers located in spare rooms, corporate high rises or Internet cafes around the world!

As a consequence, you have to be smart about how you spend your time and money. What is going to give you the biggest bang for your buck? The ubiquitous Pareto principle states that 80 percent of any effect comes from 20 percent of the causes. Also known as the law of the vital few, writing a book is one of the vital few things that you can do that can have a profound effect on the profitability of your business.

The people that best utilise this specific marketing strategy and who can reap the most professional benefit from writing a book are:

- Consultants in any field

- CEOs and business leaders

- Entrepreneurs

- Speakers and seminar presenters on any topic

- Professional services practitioners

- Training professionals

- Health practitioners

- Alternative health therapists

- Business and/or life coaches

- TV producers looking for TV tie-in products

- Anyone who has a methodology, process or proprietary technique in their area of expertise.

According to Terry H. Hill, author of *How to Jump Start Your Business* and participant in the book effectiveness study, *"If you are serious about your practice, then publishing a book is a necessity not a luxury."*

If you have been in your area of business for a number of years and have learned through trial, error and experience, then you have something valuable to say. If you have helped your clients to achieve their goals and build their business then you have something valuable to say. Writing a book offers you a way to make your intellectual capital visible to your marketplace.

Perception is important in business but that doesn't just mean shifting your customer's perception about you. It often also means shifting your perception about yourself. Sometimes the very idea of writing a book feels a little self-important or narcissistic. As a result it is often perceived as something for "other people" or perhaps a self-indulgence to consider in retirement. And, if you were considering writing your life story then unless you are Sir David Attenborough or Nelson Mandela I'd agree with you. But written and used in the right way, your book can be a potent and crucial component of your existing marketing activity.

When I graduated from university my first job was in the direct marketing department of a UK building society. I had graduated in the recession of 1992 so jobs were thin on the ground, especially for business graduates with marginal experience. Part of my job was liaising with the advertising agency and getting approval for campaigns. The business would think nothing of spending £50,000+ (US/AU $80,000+) on direct marketing campaigns every month or so.

Over my career as a marketer I've seen clients spend vast sums of money on everything from direct marketing to high finish die-cut brochures to TV and print advertising. Many with questionable results! I have a friend who works in a senior role for a global professional services company and she regularly authorises large sums of money to be spent on print advertising that doesn't produce a single response! Research shows that we don't trust advertising. According to Erik Qualman author of *Socialnomics* only 18 percent of traditional TV campaigns generate a positive return on investment and a staggering 90 percent of people skip past the adverts when they can (via Sky/TiVo/DVD). Traditional marketing is no longer working and it is unsustainable for companies – big and small – to continue to plough money into marketing that doesn't work.

You should be able to predict a significant return on investment from all your marketing activity, otherwise you shouldn't be doing it. Global powerhouses like Apple, Microsoft and Coca-Cola may be able to spend millions on brand-awareness campaigns but the vast majority of businesses don't have that financial luxury, especially not in an economic downturn.

You have to make your marketing budget work for you. It may be about time you shifted your perception and your budget away from traditional marketing with unreliable or marginal results into new marketing initiatives that can produce significantly better results at a fraction of the cost.

If you view your book as an important branding and marketing initiative, rather than an indulgent ego trip, finding the time or money may no longer be such a struggle. Writing a book is not an unnecessary expense but an important business investment.

A Word on Timing

Perhaps you're convinced. Chances are you were already pretty sold on the idea of writing your own book otherwise you wouldn't be reading this one. But perhaps you're worried about the timing. Perhaps you are reticent because the economy isn't great or your industry is struggling and you want to "wait and see". If that sounds familiar then read on...

This is the story of the hot dog seller who had the best hot dogs for miles around. He prided himself on using the very best meat, freshest rolls and a dizzying array of condiments. He had signs posted at all the intersections near his stand and knew many of his regulars by name. Business was booming. So much so that he told his son, who was studying economics, that he was going to expand. His son cautioned him, "Haven't you been reading the papers, don't be stupid, things are bad and they are going to get worse. You need to cut costs and batten down the hatches."

So the hot dog seller took his son's advice. He stopped buying the freshest rolls and bought cheaper meat. He didn't stock so many condiments and didn't bother with his signs. Sure enough business fell away! "Wow son, you are so smart – business is tough just like you predicted."

Of course, his business didn't suffer because of the economy; it suffered because he stopped doing what made him successful in the first place.

The worst thing any business can do in an economic downturn is turn their back on marketing. Sure, cut back on paper clips and Post-it notes, get everyone to turn off the lights and cut back on photocopying but marketing is an investment and never a cost.

In difficult times too many companies withdraw from the market leaving it looking like Swiss cheese! People pull back and pull out hoping to weather the storm and that leaves gaps and opportunities for those who reach out instead. Writing a book in difficult times can allow you to fill in those gaps and prosper. Besides if business is slow you've finally got the time!

If you are a busy professional, there is never going to be a "perfect time" to write your book. Now is the best time to write your book. This applies regardless of whether "now" is in a boom or bust. When the market is contracting, be bold and advance when everyone else is retreating. When the market is expanding, stake your claim on your industry and strengthen your position to better protect yourself for the inevitable contraction to follow.

Summary of Key Points

- It all sounds fabulous doesn't it! More sales, easier sales, new revenue streams, better clients, career development opportunities and credibility by the bucketload! But, is writing a book the right marketing strategy for you?

- Writing a book is a legitimate and shrewd business strategy when your business would benefit from the creation of a personal brand, what you sell is of higher value but lower volume, your business is based on creating strong customer relationships and building loyalty, your field is competitive and your business is content-rich. It is also a viable strategy if you want to expand your business or take your career in new directions, such as speaking or consulting, and if you are starting a business, rebranding or repositioning your business.

- Being good enough is no longer good enough. Unless you can reach your market then ability, skill and product ingenuity lies dormant.

- The people that best utilise this specific marketing strategy and who can reap the most professional benefit from writing a book are consultants, CEOs, business leaders, entrepreneurs, speakers and seminar presenters, professional services practitioners, training professionals, health practitioners, business and/or life coaches, TV producers looking for TV tie-in products or anyone who has a methodology, process or proprietary technique in their area of expertise.

- Writing a book offers you a way to make your intellectual capital visible to your marketplace.

- Perception is important in business but that doesn't just mean shifting your customer's perception about you. It often also means shifting your perception about yourself.

- Sometimes the very idea of writing a book feels a little self-important or narcissistic. As a result it is often perceived as something for "other people" or perhaps a self-indulgence to consider in retirement. But written and used in the right way, your book can be a potent and crucial component of your existing marketing activity.

- Over my career as a marketer I've seen clients spend vast sums of money on everything from direct marketing to high finish die-cut brochures to TV and print advertising. Many with questionable results!

- You should be able to predict a significant return on investment from all your marketing activity; otherwise you shouldn't be doing it. You have to make your marketing budget work for you. It may be about time you shifted your perception and your budget away from traditional marketing with unreliable or marginal results into new marketing initiatives that can produce significantly better results at a fraction of the cost.

- Writing a book is not an indulgent ego trip or unnecessary expense but an important business investment.

- Perhaps you're convinced. Chances are you were already pretty sold on the idea of writing your own book otherwise you wouldn't be reading this one. But perhaps you're worried about the timing. Perhaps you are reticent because the economy isn't great or your industry is struggling and you want to "wait and see".

- If you are a busy professional, there is never going to be a "perfect time" to write your book.

- Now is the best time to write your book. This applies regardless of whether "now" is in a boom or bust. When the market is contracting, be bold and advance when everyone else is retreating. When the market is expanding, stake your claim on your industry and strengthen your position to better protect yourself for the inevitable contraction to follow.

PART TWO

HOW TO WRITE YOUR BOOK

By now you will be clear about the importance and potential benefits of writing a book to establish yourself as an expert in your field, develop your personal brand, protect your intellectual property and create more, easier and more lucrative sales in your business. So let's get started.

The next four chapters deal specifically with the writing process, what you need to do to create your book and how to plan for success. At the end of each chapter there are action steps to be completed. These chapters relate to:

Days 1 – 2: Sharpen the Axe – Strategy

Days 3 – 5: Sharpen the Axe II – Structure and Substance

Days 6 – 22: Time to Write

Days 23 – 33: From Good to Great

If you encounter problems once you start writing, Chapter 12 is dedicated to helping you find solutions. If you are fully engaged with the idea of writing a book but discover that you don't enjoy writing, or can't find the time to dedicate to the task, then Chapter 13 explains the role of a ghostwriter. It covers what to look for, where to find them, what to expect and the pros and cons of hiring one.

Chapter 8

Sharpen the Axe – Strategy (Days 1 – 2)

If I had six hours to chop down a tree
I'd spend fours sharpening the axe.
~ Abraham Lincoln

Writing a book requires preparation and planning.

I once had a client who was an equities analyst and by the time we met he'd been struggling with the process of writing a book for over three years. As usual I asked to see what he'd already done and he handed over a memory stick with 19 files containing 97 separate documents! In total he'd written well in excess of 70,000 words. That is equivalent to a standard non-fiction book such as Malcolm Gladwell's *Blink: The Power of Thinking Without Thinking*. And yet he was no closer to finishing the book than he was the day he started. The content was "on paper" and it was really very good, but there was no structure, order or logic to the material. There was no start, no middle and no end. It was nothing more than a brain dump.

The key skill of a good writer is being able to connect seemingly random dots and pull structure from the chaos so that the information is unveiled in an interesting, engaging and informative way. A.A. Milne, the famous creator of Winnie-the-Pooh, said, *"Organising is what you do before you do something, so that when you do it, it is not all mixed up."*

My client's content was all mixed up simply because he didn't appreciate the importance of structure and didn't take the time, at the beginning, to clarify what he really wanted to say. Instead he made the fatal mistake of writing without a clear vision and was drowning in his own knowledge. There was no question he had the content for a really good and valuable book – but often when we know something really well, we lose perspective and can't see the proverbial wood for the trees.

I wasn't handicapped by that challenge and was able to stand in the readers' (and publishers') shoes and create a meaningful structure for the book. In this particular case, I did a first draft shuffle of information following a structure that I felt would fulfil his objectives, while also meeting the needs of the other stakeholders. This is what he had to say: *"It is amazing the difference that experience, expert knowledge, fresh eyes and a detailed understanding of what publishers want makes to a project. No wonder so many great ideas never make it into publication."*

No wonder indeed. Having a great idea is a brilliant start but if you don't spend the time planning your book you will get lost in the mire of content creation and it won't be long before "writing a book" is relegated to the "too hard basket".

What Is Your Intention?

People write books for many different reasons. Some authors are convinced they are the next J. K. Rowling and if she can become a billionaire author then so can they!

Some assume being an author will make them famous. Some just want to record a life well lived for future generations. Some want to teach and help others, using their knowledge or life lessons to inspire or warn others! And others recognise the marketing and business development opportunities that a book can provide.

What is your intention? Be honest with yourself – what do you want this book to do? Why do you want to write it? What do you believe is going to happen once you are an author? It's important to take the time to think about these issues because doing so will help you to effectively manage your expectations. I've been writing professionally since 2000 and from my experience *everyone* believes their book is special. *Everyone* believes that what they have to offer the world is unique and *everyone* will want to read it. Even though they know that most books are not bestsellers and that few people make serious money in royalties – *everyone* believes they will be the exception. *Everyone* thinks that something amazing will happen and their book will make it onto a famous book club and sell by the truckload. And at least 80 percent of the people I talk to about writing a book are adamant that they have enough material for a series of books. It never happens.

So the question you need to answer is – would you still write this book if you knew ahead of time that you would only sell a few hundred copies? If your intention is to create a book that will support your marketing and business development activity and you would write it regardless of royalty income then you are far more likely to achieve your goal and enjoy the process.

Whatever the reason, you need to be very clear why you want to write your book. You will need access to that knowledge when you experience the inevitable inertia or writer's block. You will also need to remind yourself of why you are doing it so you can beat the temptation to bump your writing duties when a more pressing task emerges. Confucius once said, *"We are so busy doing the urgent that we don't have time to do the important."*

You will always have competing demands on your time and unless you are clear about your intentions and commitments for the book then those demands will easily pull you off course. Remember, if your intention is to create a powerful business development tool to positively impact your career and increase your income then there can be few things in your professional life that can possibly take priority over that!

Know Thyself

One of the quickest and most effective ways to screw up your ambitions of becoming an author is to squash your square peg into a round hole. We are all different when it comes to how we work best. I remember when I first became a professional writer I sought advice from books on how best to create a writing business. Almost without exception those books recommended that I should set aside a certain time each day and write – no matter what. I was to get into a routine and stick to it. But I hate routine and it's probably the least productive way for me to work.

It wasn't until I wrote Paul Burgess's book about his psychometric profiling tool the I.D. System™ that I realised that there really isn't a one-size-fits-all approach to anything – including writing. I had always been puzzled by certain aspects of my nature that no matter how I tried I couldn't seem to change. For example, if someone asked me to complete a task I would say "Yes" regardless of whether I had any past experience of doing that task or not. Then I would spend several sleepless nights with sky-high blood pressure figuring it out! Invariably I'd find a way. If I'm honest it was this very characteristic that led me into writing in the first place. While writing Paul's book I looked at my own I.D. and I realised that I scored low on the "Complete" drive and particularly highly on the drive called "Improvise". This combination means that I am best suited to project based work that has a specific time frame, I love deadlines and the harder the challenge the more appealing it is. It also indicates that I become stifled by routine and my creativity and productivity drops.

By understanding myself better I was able to relax into my natural style and write the way I wanted to write. To this day I don't have a set writing routine. If I start writing and it just doesn't start flowing I leave it and go to another project or a completely different task. When the words flow easily I write for hours and, although not orthodox, I always hit the deadline.

What I discovered was that when I forced myself to write it wasn't anywhere near as good as when I just got out the way and let the words arrive on the page. Now I just trust that ability and I'm significantly more productive as a result.

You need to do the same. Find a way to write your book that works for *you*. If that means setting aside a few hours every day then do that. If that means renting a cabin by the beach for three weeks with no telephone or mobile phone access then do that.

I realise this book is called *How to Write a Book in 33 Days* but if 33 days isn't practical for you or doesn't fit with your own style of work then change it – the 33 days don't have to be consecutive! If you prefer to do a little each day, then do a little each day. If you prefer to focus on it exclusively for large chunks of time, then do that. Find *your* best way and don't listen to anyone who tells you different.

We are all unique individuals and working out how to get the best out of ourselves is a key ingredient to success in any endeavour.

Putting On Your Marketing Hat

Frank Bettger, a very successful salesman once said the quickest way to get what you want is to find out what other people want and help them get it. Writing a book follows this formula just as surely as any other marketing activity. Your book is not a platform to blow your own trumpet and talk endlessly about your achievements. No one cares! They only care about those achievements if they demonstrate your ability to solve their own challenges.

You have to keep your audience in mind from the first word to the last. That means thinking about your book from a marketing perspective. Consider:

- Who is your target market?

- What problem do you solve?

- What is your unique selling proposition (USP)?

- What benefits do you offer?

Who Is Your Target Market?

If you were conducting a traditional marketing campaign, the primary task would be to identify your target market or who you want to reach. A book is no different. Going off on pet topics or random discussions without any regard for what your reader wants is commercial suicide.

If your book is to fulfil its objective of generating new business opportunities and increasing credibility in your field, then it needs to be relevant to your target audience and address their key concerns.

Who do you want to read this book? What type of professional are you trying to appeal to? What type of new business are you trying to attract? One of the biggest mistakes you can make when writing your book is to assume everyone will want to read it or aim for a large generic "business" market.

Resist the urge to write the book as generically as possible so as to appeal to a broad readership. One-size-fits-all marketing doesn't work and it doesn't work in a book either. You may feel that you can help a wide variety of clients but it's best to focus your attention on niche groups within your broader target market.

Say, for example, you are a management consultant, and you decide that writing a book is the perfect way to differentiate yourself in a competitive market and gain new business. Potentially your target market could be anyone in business who is experiencing growth or productivity problems. It may be true that you *could* help any business regardless of industry but you will never attract potential customers with such a broad proposition. People are looking for solutions that relate more directly to them. So you need to decide who specifically you want to talk to and direct the book to that audience.

If you are unclear who your audience is or if you have several potential audiences then take a moment to consider your "ideal client". Imagine for a moment that your book is a huge success; you are inundated with new business and can't meet the demand. You are now in the enviable position of being able to pick and choose your clients. Who would you choose? Identifying your "ideal client" is more than just someone that will pay on time. What type of people and businesses do you want to work with? Have you worked with these types of people before? Think about your current clients and choose the clients you have enjoyed working with the most. Perhaps you realise that your approach is particularly effective in one or two specific industries. Perhaps you already have lucrative clients but they work in industries you feel uncomfortable about such as tobacco or weapons manufacture. You are seeking to identify the clients or potential clients that would benefit the most from what you have to offer, who would be enjoyable to work with, lucrative and aligned to your personal and professional ethics.

For example, you might look at your current client base and notice that you have several travel industry clients that you particularly enjoy working with.

It is an industry you find interesting, the clients gained some real advantage from your involvement and they paid well, without having to chase the invoices. You know as a management consultant that what you offer would be effective to any business, whether it was a travel agency or a logistics firm. But you also recognise that a marketing pitch to a generic market is a complete waste of time. People believe they are unique, and that their challenges are unique, so offering a generic approach doesn't work anymore. Clients are looking for tailor-made solutions directed to their particular industry, not blanket solutions they don't trust.

Your solution, therefore, is to write your book from a broad perspective creating the content that will be able to help any business, but use examples and case studies that relate to the travel industry and any other ideal client or niche market you've identified. That way, you don't alienate readers that don't fall into your target market while also speaking directly to those that do.

You can even direct your readers to more tailored solutions and create industry specific e-books or special reports that you can sell from your website. Remember Cialdini's principle of social proof: We are influenced to action if we can see that other people "like us" have bought something and it's been a success.

As a writer, my ideal client is an expert in their field. That field could be related to business, wealth creation, personal development, human behaviour or psychology. I prefer to work with people who are coming up with new approaches or ways of doing things that can help other people. I particularly love bringing complicated topics into the public domain so that anyone can understand and use the principles for greater success. Often my role is to act as a bridge between the expert and the reader, making the knowledge accessible while also creating a much dreamt of book for the expert.

Writing a book is a positive marketing approach for many businesses. In truth this book would also help someone wishing to write a memoir or a biography, but I've tailored the case studies and anecdotes to my ideal clients. That way it's helpful to a wide audience but especially relevant to the type of people I particularly enjoy working with.

Thinking of your target market in terms of your ideal client is a great way to focus your attention on exactly what sort of new business you are aiming for.

Not All Clients Are Good Clients

If you don't direct your writing to speak to a particular audience you still may end up with more business – but it may not be the type of new business you want!

When I returned to live in the UK from Australia, I visited several publishers in London and met with a few commissioning editors. In one of my meetings the editor quizzed me on whether I could write a particular genre of book. Apparently if I could, I'd be writing non-stop for years! She gave me a couple of books to read and asked me to get back to her. I read one of them on the way to my next appointment. The books were "misery memoirs" – stories of ordinary people who have experienced extraordinary hardship and suffering. Despite the possibility of an endless and potentially lucrative income, I just couldn't do it. Because I knew who my ideal client was and what I enjoyed writing, there was no way that I could get involved. I don't want to write books that make people feel worse about the world than they did when they started. The particular book I was given wasn't even *that* bad but it was thoroughly depressing.

Remember, not all clients are good clients. Being clear about who you want to reach and being willing to turn your back on the rest will help you to focus your message and galvanise your credibility in your target market. You probably don't have time to be all things to everyone anyway so choose your audience and market to them through specific examples. After all, life's too short for bad coffee, bad wine and pain in the ass clients!

What Problem Do You Solve?

Once you know who your target market is, and who your ideal client is, you need to find out what their fears and concerns are and address them directly throughout your book. One of the most helpful ideas I've ever come across in marketing is:

PROBLEM – AGGRAVATE – SOLVE

Your marketing should always address the challenges that your target market faces. Your book, if it's written correctly, will offer readers genuine value, while also subtly promoting your ability to solve their most pressing challenges. Your book is a very long copy sales letter! It gives the reader an opportunity to get to know you and understand you and your brand, and develop a relationship with you, whether you are aware of it or not. If it's done correctly it won't appear like a sales pitch but rather as a simple conversation with examples to help illustrate the points. It's a powerful and effective way to write.

What are your clients or prospective clients most scared of? What keeps them up at night?

You need to know what those things are, whether you are a consultant, a business coach or a motivational speaker. What does your market want?

How could you "aggravate" that problem so potential clients appreciate the urgency and importance of finding a solution? Why is your product or service a solution to that problem?

Say, for example, you are a fund manager or financial planner. Your clients are nervous and new clients are suspicious and distrustful of anyone who works in finance because of the bad press during and following the global financial crisis.

So you work out your target market and the demographic of your ideal client and you think about what those people or businesses are most scared of. You ask your current clients and find out that people are upset because of the high fees they are charged, even when the fund is not performing. You find out that people are confused and don't really understand what happened to the global financial markets. And you find out that people are scared about their future because the value of their investments has dropped significantly. Your book can address all these issues. You can then use your book to illustrate the horror stories of your industry so as to aggravate the issue and illustrate just how dangerous it can be if you don't get the right advice. You explain in plain language how the financial landscape has changed and how you are different. Illustrate those differences with examples and anecdotes from your business and incorporate testimonials and successful case studies from happy clients who used to have the same fears the reader does. Problem – Aggravate – Solve!

In the book planning stage, think about what your customer wants to read about. Find out their problems, draw attention to those challenges and their consequences. Clearly demonstrate through examples, hypothetical situations and genuine case studies that you truly understand and identify with those concerns. Use third party endorsements where possible to prove that you have the expertise and ability to help them solve those problems. Address their fears, educate them, help them and reassure them that there is a solution – you.

What Is Your USP?

Your Unique Selling Proposition (USP) is the business offer or expertise that differentiates you from other suppliers in your industry. Draw the reader's attention back to that promise and use your USP across all your marketing activity, not just your book.

If you don't know your USP and need some inspiration, start with the problems and fears you identified earlier. Going back to our financial planner, for example, he might realise that there isn't really anything that makes him different. Sure he's passionate about his business and wants to help others build wealth but that's what everyone says isn't it? He wants to set himself apart and distance himself from the bad press and lack of integrity in his industry. He knows from years of experience that one of the biggest irritations with his clients is that he receives his commissions and fees regardless of whether the investments he recommends go up or down. This irritation is now at fever pitch as story after story emerges in the press about profiteering and excessive bonuses paid at the expense of investors. Assuming this financial planner is actually one of the good guys and recommends what's right for his client, rather than what pays the biggest bonus to him, then he could differentiate himself by creating a risk reversal USP.

Risk reversal is when you remove the risk from the buying decision so that getting involved with you is a no-brainer. Domino's Pizza used this technique to turn a regional pizza store into a global brand. They recognised that the biggest irritation with home delivered pizza was that by the time it arrived it was cold. So Domino's turned that into a risk reversal USP – "Pizza delivered to your door within 30 minutes or it's free!"

Going back to our financial planner he could therefore differentiate himself by putting his money where his mouth is – WF Sample – Financial Planning – "We don't get paid unless you do!" Now I'm not an expert in financial services (and apparently neither were many of the "experts") so this may not be practical – but you get the idea! If you genuinely believe you can make a difference to your clients and help them solve their problems and achieve their dreams then take a stand and guarantee it!

My USP is speed of delivery. I also have contacts in the publishing world, which means I can often get manuscripts I've written viewed by traditional publishers if a client wishes to pursue that publishing route. Another element is my business background. I have an Honours Degree in Business and spent a decade in marketing prior to becoming a professional writer. This expertise brings a valuable dimension to my writing because I understand commercial realities and the marketing principles that people respond to. That's incredibly useful when writing a business and brand development book.

In addition, I use risk reversal. Although I've been writing professionally for over ten years and have a portfolio of books that I've written, I still guarantee my work. If a client asks me to help them with their book, no money changes hands until I have written at least one chapter so they can be assured they have found the right person for the job. I remove all the risk they may feel about whether they are making the right choice and whether I will be able to deliver the book they want.

If you can address your client's greatest fears and eradicate that fear through a delivery promise, you will set yourself apart from your competition. Then you weave those points into your book. Make a list of what makes you different and address them at appropriate times in the text. Keep reminding your reader that you can solve their challenges and you understand their concerns.

This may sound contrived but hopefully this book is a successful demonstration of the technique. Writing in this way allows you to introduce your business proposition, let the reader establish a connection to you while also delivering genuine value to the reader.

What Benefits Do You Offer?

The biggest mistake business makes is getting caught up telling their own story. Sales letters often lead with trumpet blowing gems such as, "We've been in business for 25 years!" Seriously, no one cares! They will only care once you have successfully demonstrated how that experience will benefit them. Customers will not necessarily make the mental leap between 25 years' experience and your enhanced ability to solve their problems unless you spell it out for them. It's the old features-versus-benefits argument and it's as valid in a book as it is in a marketing campaign.

Computer companies are a great example of this, with adverts such as:

Intel Celeron M530 – 1.73GHz, 533 MHz FSB 1MB L2 cache, 1GB RAM, 80GB 5400rpm, DVD-Super Multi double-layer drive, 14.1" WXGA CrystalBrite TFT LCD 1280 x 800 ExpressCard/54, 3xUSB, VGA, S-Video, Wireless 802.11b/g, built-in microphone and stereo speakers, 44.4W 6-Cell Li-ion battery, 2.6kg.

What is that all about? These may be great features but unless you understand "IT speak" then you probably have no idea what real life benefits these particular features will deliver. If, on the other hand, the computer companies advertised their products by explaining what those features gave the customer then buying a computer may be a less confusing and more enjoyable experience. For example, they could say, "Feature X means that you will be able to run at least five programs at once without affecting the speed of your machine" or "Feature Y means that your machine will start up and close down in less than 10 seconds!" That's helpful.

Don't assume people will connect the dots between the features or abilities you have and the benefits the prospective customer can achieve from those features or abilities – tell them by giving examples, success stories and third party endorsement.

If you believe in yourself and the product and service you deliver then shout it from the rooftops. There isn't much that shouts louder than a book! And you need to consider all these things BEFORE you start writing your book, not halfway through.

Action Steps

Before you start writing your book, take the time to go through this chapter and gather the information you want to get across. Specifically:

1. Look back on your working life and try to identify when you were happiest and most productive. You are looking to gain insight into the most productive way you work rather than the work you performed. Do you work better in short bursts of activity, jumping from project to project? Or do you prefer to focus on one project at a time to the exclusion of other things? Use that understanding to arrange your time to write your book.

2. Look at your current client base and record who your best clients are in whatever terms you relate to. Think of your best clients in financial terms as well as how easy and enjoyable they were to work with. Also consider whether you are interested in particular industries. Are there any correlations or similarities between your best clients?

3. Write out a full description of your ideal client and keep it visible when you are writing your book.

4. Gather testimonials and case study examples from your practice or business that illustrates your ability to deliver on your promises.

5. Write a brief position statement in bullet point form that highlights your strengths and abilities. These should relate to the characteristics and aspects of your business offering that you want to draw attention to as you write your book. Keep that visible during the writing process.

Summary of Key Points

- Writing a book requires preparation and planning.

- The key skill of a good writer is being able to connect seemingly random dots and pull structure from the chaos so that the information is unveiled in an interesting, engaging and informative way.

- Having a great idea is a brilliant start but if you don't spend the time planning your book you will get lost in the mire of content creation and it won't be long before "writing a book" is relegated to the "too hard basket".

- People write books for many different reasons – usually some combination of fame or fortune.

- What is your intention? Be honest with yourself – what do you want this book to do? Why do you want to write it?

- You will need access to that knowledge when you experience the inevitable inertia or writer's block. You will also need to remind yourself of why you are doing it so you can beat the temptation to bump your writing duties when a more pressing task emerges.

- Remember, if your intention is to create a powerful business development tool to positively impact your career and increase your income, then there can be few things in your professional life that can possibly take priority over that!

- One of the quickest and most effective ways to screw up your ambitions of becoming an author is to squash your square peg into a round hole.

- Find a way to write your book that works for *you*. If that means setting aside a few hours every day then do that. If that means renting a cabin by the beach for three weeks with no telephone or mobile phone access then do that.

- We are all unique individuals and working out how to get the best out of ourselves is a key ingredient to success in any endeavour.

- Frank Bettger, a very successful salesman, once said the quickest way to get what you want is to find out what other people want and help them get it. Writing a book follows this formula just as surely as any other marketing activity.

- If your book is to fulfil its objective of generating new business opportunities and increasing credibility in your field, then it needs to be relevant to your target audience and address their key concerns.

- Thinking of your target market in terms of your ideal client is a great way to focus your attention on exactly what sort of new business you are aiming for.

- Remember, not all clients are good clients. Life's too short for bad coffee, bad wine and pain in the ass clients!

- Once you know who your target market is, and who your ideal client is, you need to find out what their fears and concerns are and address them directly throughout your book.

- Your book, if it's written correctly, will offer readers genuine value, while also subtly promoting your ability to solve their most pressing challenges.

- Your Unique Selling Proposition (USP) is the business offer or expertise that differentiates you from other suppliers in your industry.

- Make a list of what makes you different and address them at appropriate times in the text. Keep reminding your reader that you can solve their challenges and you understand their concerns.

- Don't assume people will connect the dots between the features or abilities you have and the benefits the prospective customer can achieve from those features or abilities – tell them by giving examples, success stories and third party endorsement.

- If you believe in yourself and the product and service you deliver then shout it from the rooftops. There isn't much that shouts louder than a book! And you need to consider all these things BEFORE you start writing your book, not halfway through.

Chapter 9

Sharpen the Axe Part II – Structure and Substance (Days 3 – 5)

If you want to be a writer – stop talking about it and sit down and write!
~ Jackie Collins

The previous chapter looked at book planning from the perspective of what *you* want to get out of it. This chapter looks at how best to present the information and what information you need to present to make sure your reader feels they have bought a quality product and you meet your business development goals.

There is no point having a pet topic that you think is fascinating without any evidence that the topic is something others want to read about, knowing what you are trying to get out of the book and what aspects of your work or business you want to highlight, and how you're going to present your information.

Often when the idea to write a book finally takes hold of us, we rush to the computer or grab a notebook and start writing on a wave of enthusiasm. If you're lucky, you'll surf that wave for a week or two and create some content. The result, however, is usually nothing more than a jumble of ideas and random thoughts scattered around your home and office. You'll probably have notebooks full of ideas and scribbled messages on everything from Post-it notes to margins of newspapers to paper napkins. If this process is left unchecked, it usually isn't long before the book becomes a source of frustration and disappointment. I remember being shown one client's notes on his book and they were all stored on his computer under "The Damn Book!"

I promise you that if you don't have a plan and a structure in place before you start writing, it will never get done and the book you *never* write will haunt you. In the end, you will be so overwhelmed about how and where to start, you won't start or you will drown in your own content. You may have notes and ideas coming out your ears but if you don't find a way to structure those notes and ideas your book will remain elusive – appearing on your New Year's Resolution list year after year after year!

The critical issues you need to consider are:

- Central Premise

- Title or Working Title

- Content

- Structure

- Book Length

Central Premise

Each book will always have a variety of ideas that are explored from a variety of angles but a good book always has one, and only one, central premise. What is your central premise? There should only be one big idea in your book. In this book, for example, the central premise is that writing a book can have a significant effect on your career and income.

Everything I am saying in this book is linked to that big idea. Some of the information is providing personal and third party evidence for the idea. Some is directed toward the nuts and bolts of making that happen and providing information on how to achieve that goal. But the central premise never changes.

Having one big idea can make writing a book a whole lot easier. With a highly defined central premise all the information oozing out of your mind is streamlined around one idea or argument and this simplicity will give your writing and thinking focus. It becomes much easier to work out where information fits in your book when you know exactly what you are trying to get across in the first place.

All your information, knowledge, experience and insights will congregate around this central premise and make it easier to find a suitable structure and discard material that doesn't fit. If you don't have this central idea to guide the content you will be tempted to find ways to put everything into your book. You will cram it full of all the ideas and thoughts you've ever had whether they are genuinely relevant or not. This will detract from the message and dilute your impact.

Title or Working Title

Once you know your big idea, use it to come up with your title or at least a working title. A working title is an interim or temporary title that may be close but not quite perfect. What is your title or working title?

Your title is very important and acts like the headline or slogan in advertising. It's the thing that will get your book noticed. The most effective book titles are either self-explanatory or rely on some sort of hook or gimmick.

The title of this book is self-explanatory. *How to Write a Book in 33 Days* clearly tells potential readers what they can expect to learn from the book. Plus it emphasises that the reader can learn how to write a book quickly, which taps into my USP and is also something many people are searching for. This approach is particularly useful for non-fiction books because the title is likely to resonate with the challenge the potential reader is seeking a solution to and is likely to match or be close to what people are actually searching for. People who want to write a book, for example, but perhaps don't know how to do that or where to start will probably search the

Internet and it's highly likely that they will enter "how to write a book" or "write a book" – both appear in my title.

The other way to think of a title for your book is around your hook or gimmick – if you have one. Using a hook is especially useful when the information you are presenting is not necessarily new so the hook helps your book to stand out in a crowded genre.

For example, selling is a genre which is utterly saturated – everything of value about sales has already been written many times over. But that didn't stop sales guru Blair Singer coming up with the idea for *SalesDogs*. Assigning a breed of dog to the various personalities within sales was a brilliant hook that made it possible to cover old ground from a new perspective. It made the information fresh, interesting and funny and allowed salespeople to see that they didn't have to be a Pit Bull to be successful in their industry. *SalesDogs* became an international bestseller.

Another example is *The One Minute Manager* series. Again, everything that a manager would ever need to know about effective management has already been written many times over. The challenge, however, is that by definition many managers don't have time to trawl through management tombs – they want the information they need quickly. And that's exactly what the *One Minute Manager* series delivered and the books sold in their millions.

For most authors the idea of writing a book comes before the title but that isn't always the case. I remember meeting one guy who had come up with a genuinely brilliant title for a book so he wrote the book around that title. The book itself wasn't great, there wasn't much substance or anything of any real value but the title was so good that by the time people found out how bad it was they had already bought it! This was useful to sell books but it did nothing for his profile or credibility.

If you are writing your book for marketing and business development purposes then aim for a great title *and* great content. If you can't think of a great title then go for a self-explanatory title. It's better to write a solid value-packed book without a hook than have a clever hook and no substance.

Don't try and be too clever, complicated or cryptic. Instead make sure that either the title (or the subtitle) spells out your central premise. Let your big idea guide the title and speak directly to your audience in terms of the benefits the book will provide or the problems it will solve. Search for a title that is both descriptive and inspirational. Remember more and more people are searching for solutions online, including books. That means that the closer your book title matches what people are searching for the better.

If possible, work out what your book will be called before you start writing because it will give your writing focus and constantly bring you back to the central premise.

To be honest, I have written entire books without a title because an obvious choice just didn't "drop out" of the text, but it's never ideal. A book without a title has the tendency to deviate. In my case I ended up having to cut about 40,000 words from the finished manuscript because we went off on tangents that were, in hindsight, better suited to separate stand-alone information products such as e-books or special reports. The content wasn't wasted but the book could have been finished quicker if we had a title to direct our focus from the start.

Without a title, even just a working title, your best-case scenario is that you will veer off topic and explore rabbit holes that don't actually add value to the book. Your worst-case scenario is that you will get to the end (if you ever do) and then come up with a title and have to rework the entire book to ensure it fits the title.

Content

Once you have at least the working title and you know what your big idea is then you need to make a note of all the topics you want to cover. What is it that you actually want to say?

Many would-be authors leave this stage out because they assume they have more than enough information to write a book. That may be true, but the only way to know for sure is to work out exactly what it is you want to say.

Two things can emerge from this process. The first is that you realise that you have more than enough information in which case you need to order that information properly otherwise you may become overwhelmed and stop. Or you will discover that you actually don't have all the information you need in which case you will need to identify the gaps and do the necessary research and content development.

The best way to work out what you want to say is to map out your book using a three step process. This can either be done on computer by creating a word processing document or you can write all the bullet points on Post-it notes and create a mind map. Either way you can shuffle the ideas around until you are happy with the progression of the information. Being able to move things around easily will help to organise your thinking.

Step One: Brain Dump

Start with the end in mind. Imagine your book is finished – what information have you covered? Make a note of everything you can think of in bullet point form in the blank document.

Don't worry about whether it's right or wrong or where it will go, just make a note of everything that springs to mind when you think about your book and what you want to cover. For every bullet point consider if there is additional information under that bullet point or whether it's a stand-alone topic. Remember you are communicating to an audience that may or may not have any background information on your subject area. That means that you will need to explain everything in your book in such a way that a novice or expert could understand it and receive value.

Think top-down through your proposition as though you were explaining the entire book to a friend and make a note of all the topics you want to cover.

Think about why someone would read the book, what benefits are you offering? If you were in the market for the book you are about to write – what would you want it to contain? What specific skills or expertise do you want to get across in the book? What topics would you need to cover to answer your reader's questions? Think big picture concepts as well as any details you specifically want to cover.

Make sufficient notes so that you will remember what you meant when you revisit the document later. Don't be cryptic – if you need a paragraph to explain it, write a paragraph. No one is going to see this document. I did the brain dump for this book on the computer and it was ten pages long and wouldn't have made any sense to anyone but me.

Step Two: Order the Idea Clusters

Do any of the bullets belong together? Are there clusters of information that gather around an idea or topic? These clusters will probably form the basis of your chapters.

When you have completed the initial brain dump and moved some of the topics around, you can then expand those topics by asking yourself, "If I was reading this book what would I want to know?" Keep asking yourself this question for each idea you have.

For example, when I was running through this process for this book I asked myself what I would want to know if I was a busy professional thinking of writing a book. I realised that I would want to know what to expect so I could manage my expectations. I would want to know the benefits writing a book could deliver. I'd also want to know about the publishing options available to me and their respective advantages and disadvantages. Every time I thought of something else I would simply make a new bullet point and add it to my document.

This doesn't have to be perfect; the objective is to make a note of all the things you want to discuss. Initially, that may simply be chapter headings and sections, but you will have to drill down to come up with the details you want to present. You may find that the same ideas come under different topic headings. In that situation, put the idea under each topic it relates to. When you start writing, explain the idea in full the first time you reference it and then just refer back to it later in the book. For example, the work of Robert Cialdini is relevant under many topics in this book. I introduced his work in Chapter 1 and then refer back to him later in the book. I don't need to keep explaining who he is or what he's written because it's covered earlier.

Once you have all the topics, it may become obvious that you have to shuffle the order of your chapters. For example, I thought that explaining the publishing options was important but I thought it probably wasn't as important as explaining the benefits of writing a book in the first place.

These things soon become obvious when you work through your idea in this way. Use this process to create an outline of your book and fully engage in the progression of the argument. Read your shuffled chapters out loud and "talk through your case". Keep asking yourself, "What does my reader need to know now?" Take each concept and drill into the detail as much as you can.

Each chapter will follow the same format – start with the big idea of *that* chapter and then drill down into the detail so that the reader gets a thorough and logical understanding of the topic.

Step Three: Create the Table of Contents

The objective of the first two steps is to get you ready to create your Table of Contents. This Table of Contents will then become the skeleton of the book and you then flesh out the ideas into the relevant chapters.

Not only will this make the writing process much easier, and hopefully more enjoyable, but if you want a mainstream publisher then you will need to provide this with your proposal and a few sample chapters. You will therefore need to create this Table of Contents eventually anyway so better do it early and let it guide your book development.

If you have done step one and two on Post-it notes and a whiteboard it's time to transfer your ideas and topic clusters to a word processing document. If you have already created a document then create a "save as" version of your expanded brain dump document and start creating chapter titles, headings and subsections from this document.

Don't worry about populating these areas yet, just list them one after another in one central document. Leave a few spaces between each one and make sure you format the text into either "Heading 1", "Heading 2" or "Heading 3".

These heading conventions are important for ordering the information and they will remain important right through to publication. Level one headings indicate a top level topic, if there is additional information to be discussed under that topic those discussions should appear under a level two heading. If the level two heading also has additional content then present *that* information under a level three heading. Headings help your reader to understand where they are and what they are going to learn. It guides them through the material by helping them to identify what topics are connected and what topics are entirely new. Three heading levels are sufficient for most books. In this book I've used level one headings for chapter headings, level two headings for section headings and finally level three headings for subsections. Depending on the depth of your material you may need to have a chapter heading which is distinct from the level one, two and three headings. You can modify the settings for those headings on your own computer to choose the font and point size.

Once you have attributed a heading level to each new section of material most word processing packages will automatically generate your Table of Contents. For example, when I was creating the framework for this chapter I had a list of bullet points which were then given appropriate headings and when Microsoft Word automatically created the Table of Contents the section relating to this chapter looked like this...

- Chapter 9: Sharpen the Axe Part II – Structure and Substance (Days 3 – 5) *Heading 1*

  o Central Premise *Heading 2*

  o Title or Working Title *Heading 2*

  o Content *Heading 2*

    ▪ Step One: Brain Dump *Heading 3*

- Step Two: Order the Clusters *Heading 3*

- Step Three: Create the Table of Contents H*eading 3*

o Structure *Heading 2*

o Book Length *Heading 2*

Once you have a list of your headings in the appropriate format simply generate your Table of Contents and you're almost ready to start. It's important to appreciate that this initial Table of Contents *will* change. As you get into the detail and start writing the content you will realise that the odd idea is in the wrong place or that you've missed something or need to delete something. So long as you adhere to the heading conventions that you start with then you can refresh the Table of Contents in a few seconds and continue with the new framework. The purpose of this exercise is to give you a writing guide and keep you on track to a finished product. It's an essential step if you want to turn your dream of becoming an author into reality.

Structure

When you first think of writing a book you may be tempted to think that the content is the most important issue. It's not. Finding the right structure or context for your content is, by far, the most important aspect of any book. If you get the structure right, no one will even notice it and the book will become effortless to read. Add that to great content and you've got a winner because your book will progress logically and clearly while constantly inviting the reader to move to the next section. If you get the structure wrong, even if the content is brilliant your book will require real effort to finish and all but your most committed readers will give up.

Our minds are fairly linear. We like things to be in a certain order and when they are not it is confusing. Confusion is the fastest way to disengage a reader and confused readers don't contact the author for assistance. If you want your book to be a glowing advertisement of your work and ability you need to make it clear, engaging and valuable.

There are many ways you could potentially structure the information you want to share. Often the title of the book or the hook you choose will influence the structure you choose and the chapter titles. For example in Stephen Covey's *The 7 Habits of Highly Effective People* – the hook is 7 Habits. Therefore the structure of the book mirrors these habits and each chapter discusses one of the habits. This is a simple, effective and logical structure.

If your book is going to explain your process or methodology then the most logical structure would be to identify the discrete parts of that process or methodology and explain each part in a separate chapter. This way you lead the reader through the information in a logical sequence so they can understand the material.

When you are deciding about structure you need to think about your audience. This is why knowing your target market is so important. Never write a book to a market, write a book to one individual and know who that person is. Think about how that person would like to progress through the information.

Most people learn best when the information they need to learn is presented in a logical sequence from big ideas down through the detail, using examples and case studies to bring the information to life through real world examples. The structure you choose should therefore allow the reader to accumulate knowledge as they progress through the book.

Many people have tried to write their book using the parable structure made popular by *Who Moved My Cheese* by Dr Spencer Johnson (co-author of the *One Minute Manager* series). This is a difficult book style to get right and you must be an effective storyteller to pull it off. It's also not a particularly effective structure if you are seeking to showcase your knowledge and expertise. It's definitely useful to add stories to your book of real world application of your methodology or process, but don't assume that your potential customer will make the mental leap between a parable and your ability to solve their problems.

Book Length

I'm often asked how long a book should be. The simple answer is that your book should be as long as it needs to be to say what you need to say and not a word over that. But I appreciate that's not terribly helpful.

If what you are seeking to create is your "legacy book" i.e. you plan to write one really great book which will be your legacy to the world then you should be aiming for 70,000 – 100,000 words. Malcolm Gladwell's *Blink* is just over 70,000 words whereas Stephen Covey's *7 Habits of Highly Successful People* is just over 100,000. If you are creating your legacy book then it needs to look substantial. Remember perception is everything in business. If you hand over your book to a potential client and it's little more than a pamphlet then it will not have the same weight or significance as it would if it thumps down on the desk.

Of course, word count is not the only way that you can create a significant looking book but if you make the font unnaturally large or have too much white space you'll just shoot yourself in the foot.

The two most frequently used formats for non-fiction are B-format and Demy. The dimensions of a B-format book, also known as trade paperback, is 198 x 129 mm (8 x 5 1/4 in). Malcolm Gladwell's books are created in B-format as is *Freakonomics* by Steven D. Levitt & Stephen J. Dubner or *Drive* by Daniel Pink. It's the format often used for paperback bestsellers. The dimensions of Demy, also known as US Trade, are up for debate with different places quoting different dimensions but the most popular is 229 x 125 mm (9 x 6 in). This format is used for general non-fiction including business and self-help in hardback and paperback format.

The other option that can still work as a brand building tool is the smaller 40,000 word book. As discussed the *Who Moved My Cheese* or *One Minute Manager* series are smaller books that have worked well both in terms of book sales and credibility. Seth Godin's *Purple Cow* is actually just over 30,000 words. This format is popular, probably because we have less and less time to read a book. This size can sometimes work well if your process isn't too complex or if you want to create a practical guide book or tool that your customers would refer back to often.

However, if you have the material, the larger legacy book will always have more marketing and business development impact.

The other major concern for many would-be authors is how much information to reveal in the book. The thinking is something like this, "If I reveal all my secrets then why would the reader contact me for advice or future help?" On the face of it, this is a valid argument but don't be tempted to hold back.

Even if you did give your reader every secret and trick of the trade, the fact is that most people don't find it easy to transfer ideas into action without assistance. For example, I have a client who is the CEO of a business and executive coaching firm. We've written two books together and both contain very detailed descriptions of the methodology he uses and why it works. He provides step by step instructions on how to use the techniques to achieve outstanding performance. The client or potential client therefore has the knowledge for the cost of a book and yet many prefer to hire his firm to facilitate the process for thousands of dollars, often hundreds of thousands of dollars!

How many great ideas have you read about but never implemented? This happens all the time. Just look at the seminar industry for example. Participants bounce from one new-age guru to the next, some even returning time and again to the same seminar and yet nothing actually changes. The reason isn't because those people are unmotivated or lazy. It's because, contrary to popular belief, turning an idea into a reality is a skill that few people possess. We usually need a framework, support or one-on-one guidance to make long-lasting change.

The other important consideration is that you really do need to give value and you need to demonstrate your ability in your field – especially if your objective is to use the book as a business card. I was reminded of this principle while watching the second series of *The Restaurant*. This is a UK TV show where nine couples compete to win the right to open a restaurant with legendary Michelin Star chef Raymond Blanc. The couples are each given a restaurant to run and each week one couple is eliminated after they all complete a challenge. One week the task was to give a cookery demonstration at a chosen venue. One of the couples were given a rowing regatta as their venue and produced what looked like beautiful food. The problem was, they wouldn't let anyone taste it! Their logic was that if the people watching the demonstration liked the look of the food, they would book a table for dinner. Guess how many bookings they made? Not one – and that's the same response you can expect from your book if you don't allow people to sample your product or service.

I thoroughly recommend giving everything you have and a little bit more, especially in the first draft. If you find your book is over 100,000 words long then you might want to think about cutting it back or you may decide to remove certain sections and turn them into special reports or value-add products.

The reality is that if you want your book to work as a marketing and business development tool you must demonstrate your expertise and that means that you *will* have to "give away" some of your trade secrets. Some may take the knowledge from your book and use it for themselves without needing you further – and that should be a source of pride for you. The rest will hopefully think of you when they are in the market for your services, pull down your book from the shelf and give you a call.

And if you're worried about people stealing your material, protect it wherever possible through trademarks etc. Besides, you've written the book so it's obvious your material came first and you'll be able to prove that if things turn ugly. After that just remember that imitation is the highest form of flattery and move on.

A book should be the length it needs to be in order to say what you need to say. Don't pad it out. Keep the writing tight, strong and focused on adding value. See how long it naturally ends up being and let the content decide.

Action Steps

Before you start writing your book, take the time to go through this chapter and gather the information you want to present. Specifically:

1. What is the central premise of your book? What big idea are you trying to get across?

2. Come up with five possible titles around this central premise and choose the one that most clearly tells the reader what benefits they can expect to gain from reading your book. This is your "working title".

3. Do you have a clever hook that could help you stand out – especially if your content has been thoroughly covered by other authors?

4. Follow the three steps to map out your book and create a detailed Table of Contents.

Summary of Key Points

- This chapter looks at how best to present the information and what information you need to present to make sure your reader feels they have bought a quality product and you meet your business development goals.

- The second element of the planning stage deals specifically with structure and substance, and the critical issues you need to consider are the central premise, title or working title, content, structure and book length.

- Each book will always have a variety of ideas that are explored from a variety of angles but a good book always has one, and only one, central premise.

- With a highly defined central premise all the information oozing out of your mind is streamlined around one idea or argument and this simplicity will give your writing and thinking focus.

- Once you know your big idea, use it to come up with your title or at least a working title. A working title is an interim or temporary title that may be close but not quite perfect.

- The most effective book titles are either self-explanatory or rely on some sort of hook or gimmick.

- Don't try and be too clever, complicated or cryptic. Instead make sure that either the title (or the subtitle) spells out your central premise.

- If possible work out what your book will be called before you start writing because it will give your writing focus and constantly bring you back to the central premise.

- Without a title you will veer off topic and explore rabbit holes that don't actually add value to the book, never finish, or have to rework the entire book to ensure it fits with the title you eventually decide on.

- Once you have at least the working title and you know what your big idea is then you need to make a note of all the topics you want to cover.

- The best way to work out what you want to say is to map out your book using a three step process – brain dump, order the idea cluster and create a Table of Contents.

- This can either be done on computer by creating a word processing document or you can write all the bullet points on Post-it notes and create a mind map. Being able to move things around easily will help to organise your thinking.

- Start with the end in mind. Imagine your book is finished – what information have you covered? Make a note of everything you can think of in bullet point form in the blank document.

- Do any of the bullets belong together? Are there clusters of information that gather around an idea or topic? These clusters will probably form the basis of your chapters.

- When you have completed the initial brain dump and moved some of the topics around, you can then expand those topics by asking yourself, "If I was reading this book what would I want to know?" Keep asking yourself this question for each idea you have.

- Once you have all the topics, it may become obvious that you have to shuffle the order of your chapters.

- The objective of the first two steps is to get you ready to create your Table of Contents. This Table of Contents will then become the skeleton of the book and you then flesh out the ideas into the relevant chapters.

- Start creating chapter titles, headings and subsections from the document.

- Don't worry about populating these areas yet, just list them one after another in one central document. Leave a few spaces between each one and make sure you format the text into either "Heading 1", "Heading 2" or "Heading 3".

- Once you have a list of your headings in the appropriate format simply generate your Table of Contents and you're almost ready to start.

- When you first think of writing a book you may be tempted to think that the content is the most important issue. It's not. Finding the right structure or context for your content is, by far, the most important aspect of any book.

- Never write a book to a market, write a book to one individual and know who that person is. Think about how that person would like to progress through the information.

- The structure you choose should therefore allow the reader to accumulate knowledge as they progress through the book.

- Your book should be as long as it needs to be to say what you need to say and not a word over that.

- If what you are seeking to create is your "legacy book" i.e. you plan to write one really great book which will be your legacy to the world, then you should be aiming for 70,000 – 100,000 words.

- The two most frequently used formats for non-fiction are B-format and Demy.

- The other option that can still work as a brand building tool is the smaller 40,000 word book. This size can sometimes work well if your process isn't too complex or if you want to create a practical guide book or tool that your customers would refer back to often.

- However, if you have the material, the larger legacy book will always have more marketing and business development impact.

- The other major concern for many would-be authors is how much information to reveal in the book. Don't be tempted to hold back.

- Even if you did give your reader every secret and trick of the trade, the fact is that most people don't find it easy to transfer ideas into action without assistance.

- We usually need a framework, support or one-on-one guidance to make long-lasting change.

- Plus you really do need to give value and you need to demonstrate your ability in your field – especially if your objective is to use the book as a business card.

- I thoroughly recommend giving everything you have and a little bit more, especially in the first draft.

- Don't pad it out. Keep the writing tight, strong and focused on adding value. See how long it naturally ends up being and let the content decide.

Chapter 10
Time to Write (Days 6 – 22)

The writer does the most good who
gives his reader the most knowledge
and takes from him the least time.
~ Sydney Smith

By now you should be clear about what you want to achieve from writing your book. You should have thought about your audience from a marketing perspective and worked out what their biggest challenges and fears are and how you can solve them. You should have clarified your central premise, created a detailed Table of Contents including chapter headings, section headings and subsections, together with a list of bullet points of what you want to cover.

Now all you need to do is take a section at a time and write.

Whatever you can do or dream you can, begin it.
Boldness has genius, power and magic in it.
~ Goethe

I appreciate that this may sound deceptively simple but if you've followed the advice from previous chapters you will find it much easier than you imagined. The detailed road map created by the Table of Contents will not only make the process easier, but may even make the entire journey fun!

Often what makes writing so hard is not the writing itself, it's the not knowing what to write! With the Table of Contents as your blueprint, that challenge is significantly overcome. Granted, you still have to write, but at least you have a structure to follow and that can make all the difference.

The Hallmarks of Powerful Writing

There are whole books dedicated to good writing – I certainly have a few in my library although I have to confess I haven't read many of them! One of the most important lessons I ever learnt about writing came in a course I did many years ago. At the time, one of my writing clients was a seminar company that specialised in Neuro Linguistic Programming (NLP), a type of personal development, and I was offered a ticket to a writing workshop. Never one to turn down a free ticket to a seminar, I went along.

At the end of the first day we were asked to bring in a piece of writing that we loved so we could share it with the group. I rarely read fiction but chose the following passages from Kurt Vonnegut's *Mother Night*.

"I have never seen a more sublime demonstration of the totalitarian mind, a mind which might be likened unto a system of gears whose teeth have been filed off at random. Such a snaggle-toothed thought machine, driven by a standard, or even substandard libido, whirls with the jerky, noisy, gaudy pointlessness of a cuckoo clock in Hell.

The dismaying thing about the classic totalitarian mind is that any given gear, though mutilated, will have at its circumference unbroken sequences of teeth that are immaculately maintained, that are exquisitely machined. The missing teeth, of course, are simple, obvious truths, truths available and comprehensible even to ten-year-olds, in most cases.

I have never tampered with a single tooth in my thought machine, such as it is. There are teeth missing, God knows – some I was born without, teeth that will never grow. And other teeth have been stripped by the clutchless shifts of history. But never have I willfully destroyed a tooth on a gear of my thinking machine. Never have I said to myself, "This fact I can do without."

I love this passage. I'm not sure why – I just love it. I think it's smart, provocative and insightful. I assumed that others would share my awe at Vonnegut's evident genius. It didn't happen. I couldn't believe the variety of reaction from the group... Some people thought he must have been depressed when he wrote it. Others thought he was angry. Some loved it. Some hated it. Some didn't "get it". I just thought it was an extraordinary piece of writing!

I realised in that moment that if opinion could be so divided about one of the greatest writing talents of our time then what possible chance have the rest of us got! This revelation offered me a priceless insight and taught me a very valuable lesson – writing is a purely subjective experience.

I would suggest that you accept that fact right now. There will be people that absolutely love your book. I am, of course, hoping that there will be people, perhaps even you, that will absolutely love *this* book but I'm also realistic enough to know that there will also be people that hate it with a passion! The same is true of your book. You can't please all of the people all of the time – everyone brings their own experience, ideas, personal philosophies, attitudes and outlooks to everything they do and those things colour their experience. A book is no different. So my heartfelt advice is: please yourself. Create a book that you are genuinely proud of and let it go. If you can stand back and say, "Yes, I wrote that and it was the best I could do at that time," then be happy. You can't control how it will be received.

Plus, what this revelation means is that if opinion about what constitutes good writing is so varied there can't possibly be any cast iron rules on how to do it. There are, however, some hallmarks to great writing. Those hallmarks are:

1. Select an Appropriate Voice and Style

2. Be Specific

3. Don't Use Jargon

4. Write as You Speak

5. Make Your Writing Accessible

6. Have Your Research Ready

7. Suspend Your Judgement

1. Select an Appropriate Voice and Style

*There's one thing your writing must have to be
any good at all. It must have you. Your soul,
your self, your heart, your guts, your voice – you
must be on every page... So dare to be yourself.
Dare to reveal yourself. Be honest, be
open, be true... If you are, everything
else will fall into place.
~ Elizabeth Ayres*

Let yourself be seen in the pages of your book by selecting an appropriate voice and style. In the opening chapter, we explored the value of branding and how writing a book could facilitate the creation of a personal brand. This is especially true when you put yourself into the book. This honesty is refreshing and it also allows the reader to establish if they like you and resonate with your brand values and your message.

Some people shy away from putting their heart on their sleeve and how far you go will depend on your industry and your personality. I believe you should allow your personality to come through because it gives the reader some insight into you and your business. We may like to think we are logical, rational creatures and that business is an entity and we conduct our affairs in some orderly mechanistic fashion, but we are human beings first. Businesses are collections of human beings. And the truth is that perfect service and exceptional quality delivered by someone you dislike or find offensive will usually lose out to someone with good service and solid quality that is a pleasure to work with.

So allow someone to see you. Besides, wouldn't you rather work with clients that like you, respect your message and are excited about how you could help them?

I am well aware that some people may read this book and have no interest in contacting me – even if they are desperately looking for a ghostwriter. I'm sure some people will think I'm a little too informal and perhaps a little too blunt. But I'm okay with that and you should be too. Be yourself.

This process is greatly assisted if you write from your point of view in the first and second person (I/we and you). This style of writing is more active and reaches out to the reader in a one-to-one conversation that is far more engaging. If you have an opinion or a theory that you are convinced could help others then tell people, stick your neck out and take ownership of the theory through your words.

Ironically, I think this is especially true in the usually insipid world of business books. Far from being a bland passive treatise of your ideas, it should be obvious to those who know you well that you wrote the book. If you are sarcastic in real life don't be afraid to put sarcasm in your book (although don't overdo it!). If you are direct or subtle let your writing reflect those qualities. Your book should be a reflection of your personality, your ethics and your values. Remember, a book offers readers the chance to get to know you and what you stand for. They will use that information to decide whether they like you or not and whether they agree with your ideas.

People do business with people they like and people "like them". So if you want your book to generate new business opportunities, isn't it better that you attract people that resonate with your authentic message rather than trying to please everyone?

You may alienate some people but it doesn't matter. You can't work with everyone anyway so let your personality come through in your writing. Don't be controversial just for the sake of it, and don't be rude or libellous, but make your mark so that readers get a glimpse at the person behind the pages.

2. Be Specific

Don't hide behind passive language and don't waffle. Generalities are weak, so when you are explaining your theory, or what you can bring to a business, use detailed examples. Use case studies that have occurred in your own business. Not only does this give you a chance to showcase your work without sounding like a blowhard but it lets your reader get a deeper understanding of the message.

If you have a theory, methodology or approach that you want to share, then explaining the various elements or stages of that process is important but it can easily become dull and one-dimensional. If you weave examples and real world scenarios into those explanations you bring life to the book whilst also aiding comprehension because the reader can see how the theory works in practice.

The reason that metaphor and analogies are so powerful is because they often illuminate a concept and make it easier to understand. If you explain a challenging topic by attaching a "known" to an "unknown", you allow the reader to gain a greater and faster appreciation of your ideas. When they can read how the theory or approach works in business they get a larger and more holistic appreciation for what you are saying.

Wherever possible, validate your ideas with research and third party verification. If you know of a study that backs up your philosophy then accurately reference that study. Not only does this properly acknowledge the findings of the research, it adds weight and credibility to your writing. When the reader is helped to understand your point of view whilst also being reassured that it's not *just* your point of view then they gain confidence in your perspective. Referencing corroborating theories is much more credible and therefore more powerful.

Another popular way to verify opinion is through the use of quotations from appropriate well-known figures from history. If you make a statement about the importance of thinking, for example, and add a quotation from Albert Einstein that supports your opinion then you lean on the credibility of Einstein. Borrowing credibility from famous thinkers allows you to endorse your own thinking by people better known than you whilst also providing a good way to break up large blocks of text.

3. Don't Use Jargon

If there is jargon or technical terminology in your industry then explain the terms as simply as possible the first time you use them and keep their use to an absolute minimum. Often jargon is simply a form of intellectual snobbery and while you may end up looking clever, the book will be a failure. Preaching to the converted so you can feel intellectually superior won't win you new business. If your objective is to get your message across to a new audience then you have to explain yourself in lay terms. That doesn't mean dumbing your book down – it just means that you have to be clear, precise and understandable.

Jargon is basically a shortcut to understanding for those within an industry. If you are seeking to attract people from outside that industry then you need to unpack that shortcut so they understand what you are talking about. Plus there is nothing more boring than reading a book full of acronyms where you have to stop and think about the acronym before you can understand and move on.

In the same vein, don't overly complicate the language. George Orwell once said, *"Never use a long word when a short one will do."* And Orwell was hardly a literary slouch.

Make sure you don't have to reread any sections in order to understand them. Instead, rewrite them until they flow easily and the meaning is clear and obvious.

4. Write as You Speak

It's unclear where the pomposity of business communication came from. Perhaps it is a throwback from the British Empire. Perhaps it's just a facade to hide behind to avoid taking any real responsibility for what's being said. Perhaps it's a form of one-upmanship. Whatever the reason, it's extremely dull to read and has done a great disservice to writing.

A brilliant demonstration of just how much of a disservice can be read in William Zinsser's classic book on non-fiction writing, *On Writing Well*. Zinsser refers to this penchant in business writing to be stiff, laborious and lacking in humanity and uses a famous verse by Ecclesiastes and a business translation into "business speak" by the great George Orwell to demonstrate the point brilliantly!

Ecclesiastes:

"I returned and saw under the sun, that the race is not to the swift, nor the battle to the strong, neither yet bread to the wise, nor riches to men of understanding, nor yet favour to men of skill; but time and chance happeneth to them all."

Orwell:

"Objective consideration of contemporary phenomena compels the conclusion that success or failure in competitive activities exhibits no tendency to be commensurate with innate capacity, but that a considerable element of the unpredictable must invariably to taken into account."

Zinsser comments, *"Gone from the second one are the short words and vivid images from everyday life – the race and the battle, the bread and the riches – and in their place have waddled the long and flabby nouns of generalised meaning. Gone is any sense of what one person did ("I returned") or what he realised ("saw") about one of life's central mysteries: the capriciousness of fate."*

If your mission is to inform, educate and inspire your reader then steer clear of the latter style of writing. Forget trying to be too stiff; don't even worry too much about your grammar and spelling at the early stages and instead just focus on getting your message and personality across.

Write as though you were having a spoken conversation with a friend. For example, use contractions instead of writing out the words in full. No one says, "I cannot drive the bus." They say "I can't drive the bus."

When you are reading your book, it should sound conversational. Don't limit your readership by using words and phrases that only mean certain things to certain people. Remember your potential readership is global so make sure you are clear in your explanations without using colloquial language.

5. Make Your Writing Accessible

Have you ever opened a book and been faced with solid text? If you have you will probably remember you closed it pretty soon afterwards. Don't over-elaborate your writing and extend paragraphs into longwinded blocks of text. People are in a hurry to get to the information they need, so make your writing accessible and easy to read and navigate.

Vary the length of your sentences and paragraphs to make reading more interesting. If a sentence reaches 20+ words, consider breaking it down into two sentences. Vary the length and don't get too hung up about grammatical laws. For example, the grammar police will say you can't start a sentence with "And" or "But". But, as you can see, sometimes it is very effective for making an additional point. Even very short sentences have their place and can add impact to your writing.

Another way to break up large chunks of text is to use effective headings and subheadings. This also aids comprehension because it helps the reader to know where they are and what to expect from the section.

Readers come in all shapes and sizes – there are those that have never read a book from cover to cover in their life. There are those that insist on reading every word and will often read the same book several times. You have to cater for as many reader types as possible. The "grazer", for example, will enjoy being able to open a book and pick and choose the bits that interest them based on bullet points and headings. Dividing your book up into appropriate and logical sections helps the reader easily find what they are looking for.

Accessibility can also be greatly assisted in the design and layout stage. White space is very important because it gives the reader a breather. A good designer will know the importance of white space when laying out your book. Nothing is more unappealing than large blocks of uninterrupted text.

6. Have Your Research Ready

If you have done research on your topic or have gathered articles or references over the years that you feel may be useful, have all the material handy. If you plan to refer to certain books then have access to them. Having the research material you need close at hand can ensure that you don't get sidetracked while you go and find a piece of information.

If you are writing and you find yourself thinking of a fact, figure, reference or quote that you want to use but don't have it to hand, just make a note to remind you. Write the note in block capitals and change the text colour to red. That way you don't interrupt the writing process and get sidetracked for hours while you try to find a tiny bit of content. Don't be cryptic – write as full a description as you'll need to remind yourself later what you wanted to add in that spot.

Once you have your first draft manuscript, go through the manuscript and find all the red text sections and fill in the blanks. Once you have found your reference or extra piece of information and added it seamlessly into the text, change the text colour back to black and move on to the next missing reference.

7. Suspend Your Judgement

The final hallmark of great writing is learning to suspend you judgement about the value or quality of your writing – at least until you have the basic content in place. Accept that it's not going to be perfect first time around. It won't flow from you in its finished form. And some people will always hate it!

Give yourself the freedom to write. If you don't allow yourself this freedom then you run the very real risk of "analysis paralysis" or "performance anxiety" – both of which usually herald the death knell of any author ambitions you may have.

Just write!

Your only job at this stage is to follow the structure you've created and populate the Table of Contents. Polish and perfection comes much later.

Additional Ideas to Consider

Over the years I've come across umpteen tips and tricks to use as a writer. Most of them have been utterly useless for me. But we are all different. Here are a couple of things I do use that have proved both enjoyable and useful.

Carry a Dedicated Notebook

Once you start the writing process you will probably be surprised to discover it's never far from your mind. Consequently you are likely to have some good ideas at the most inappropriate times. Buy a notebook dedicated to the project and take it everywhere you go.

I have learnt through experience that no matter how convinced you are that you will remember the idea that's suddenly sprung to mind at 4 am, chances are you won't. So leave the notebook on the bedside table at night together with a pen and a torch. Turning the bedside light on and off like a 1960s disco all night can be extremely irritating for your partner, so the torch offers a discreet alternative. Whatever you do, record your flashes of insight otherwise you may kick yourself in the morning.

Record Your Thoughts

Recording your thoughts is also a great way to turn over ideas and record new insights. You can either buy a Dictaphone or just use your mobile phone. If you have a smart phone you can even download a voice recognition application and have your voice converted to text automatically. Even if you don't have a smart phone, even the old bricks have a record function. This can be especially useful if you are driving or are in a situation where you can't write your ideas down.

I find that a lot of my best ideas come to me when I'm doing something else, especially if I am free to talk to myself at the same time! I know it sounds a bit nutty but my best thinking occurs when I'm able to verbalise it. So if I'm out for a walk in the country or driving somewhere I often talk to myself about the project I'm working on, going over my ideas and theories out loud. If I'm walking then I keep a notebook and record what springs to mind and if I'm driving I just set the record button on my phone and pretend I'm on hands-free!

Talk Your Book

Dictating your entire book is also a great way to gather content. Some people find it much easier to talk than to write. If that is the case for you, then you should consider talking your book into a recording device.

I would still recommend that you create the detailed Table of Contents to start with but use that structure to dictate your book and create audio files. Then simply transcribe the recordings and you will have the bulk of your content.

Read!

One of the best ways to become a better writer is to become a better reader. Not only are you always expanding your knowledge base, but you get the opportunity to see what works and what doesn't.

Look at books you have enjoyed reading and see if there are any clues as to why. For example, I like books that summarise the key points at the end of every chapter. I originally saw this done in Napoleon Hill's *Think and Grow Rich* and I found it a useful tool which I have used for many books I've written including this one. It's particularly useful for the "grazer" reader who doesn't necessarily want to read the whole book but wants to quickly get to the key points.

If you read widely you are likely to start pulling in ideas from odd and interesting sources that you may never have considered until the moment when you were called to explain your ideas in print.

Action Steps

As you begin to write, take the time to go through this chapter and direct your writing using the hallmarks identified above. Specifically.

1. What positive aspects of your character do you want to bring out in your writing, for example, integrity, precision or sense of humour?

2. If you have relevant third party independent evidence you may need written permission to quote from the study. Kick that process off immediately.

3. Make a list of all the jargon in your industry so that you are reminded to explain it fully when using it in your book.

4. Collect all your research material in one place. That means all the books you may reference, newspaper articles and industry journals. That way you can slot it in as you write without interrupting your writing flow.

5. Buy a notebook and record your random thoughts about the book. Or work out how to use the record function of your mobile phone.

6. Go to a good bookshop or hop online and find competitor books that look as though they may cover what you wish to discuss. Buy the best ones and read them.

Summary of Key Points

- Now it's time to write.

- This may sound deceptively simple but the detailed road map created by the Table of Contents will not only make the process easier, but may even make the entire journey fun!

- Writing is a purely subjective experience.

- If opinion about what constitutes good writing is so varied there can't possibly be any cast iron rules on how to do it.

- There are, however, some hallmarks to great writing. Those hallmarks are: select an appropriate voice and style, be specific, don't use jargon, write as you speak, make your writing accessible, have your research ready and suspend your judgement.

- Let yourself be seen in the pages of your book by selecting an appropriate voice and style.

- This process is greatly assisted if you write from your point of view in the first and second person (I/we and you).

- Don't hide behind passive language and don't waffle. Generalities are weak, so when you are explaining your theory, or what you can bring to a business, use detailed examples.

- Validate your ideas with research and third party verification.

- Another popular way to verify opinion is through the use of quotations from appropriate well-known figures from history.

- If there is jargon or technical terminology in your industry then explain the terms as simply as possible the first time you use them and keep their use to an absolute minimum.

- In the same vein, don't overly complicate the language. George Orwell once said, *"Never use a long word when a short one will do."* And Orwell was hardly a literary slouch.

- Forget trying to be too stiff; don't even worry too much about your grammar and spelling at the early stages and instead just focus on getting your message and personality across.

- Don't over-elaborate your writing and extend paragraphs into longwinded blocks of text. People are in a hurry to get to the information they need, so make your writing accessible and easy to read and navigate.

- Accessibility can also be greatly assisted in the design and layout stage. White space is very important because it gives the reader a breather.

- If you have done research on your topic or have gathered articles or references over the years that you feel may be useful, have all the material handy.

- Having the research material you need close at hand can ensure that you don't get sidetracked while you go and find a piece of information.

- The final hallmark of great writing is learning to suspend you judgement about the value or quality of your writing – at least until you have the basic content in place.

- Once you start the writing process you will probably be surprised to discover it's never far from your mind. Buy a notebook and take it everywhere you go or use the record function on your mobile to ensure you never forget any ideas.

- Some people find it much easier to talk than to write. If that is the case for you, then you should consider talking your book into a recording device.

- Then simply transcribe the recordings and you will have the bulk of your content.

- One of the best ways to become a better writer is to become a better reader. Not only are you always expanding your knowledge base, but you get the opportunity to see what works and what doesn't.

- If you read widely you are likely to start pulling in ideas from odd and interesting sources that you may never have considered until the moment when you were called to explain your ideas in print.

Chapter 11
From Good to Great
(Days 23 – 33)

In every fat book there is a thin
book trying to get out.
~ Anon

If you have followed the process laid out in the previous chapters you should now have a rough first draft manuscript.

Chances are that once you got going you surprised yourself about just how much you know about your industry. Hopefully you also enjoyed writing. Bill Wheeler once said, *"Good writing is clear thinking made visible."* William Zinsser said, *"Writing is thinking on paper."* Often it is only when we seek to explain a subject to another that we fully appreciate our own knowledge in that area. The writing process clarifies our thought process. This is why writing a book can be such a valuable exercise for developing the intellectual capital in your business and formalising IP.

Filling in the Table of Contents will no doubt have illustrated just how true that is. Getting the bulk of the content down onto paper is a huge piece of the puzzle. But the most important part is still to come.

Apply the Polish

Turning the base content into a book requires attention to eight editing essentials so that you can apply the polish to your manuscript. These are not necessarily aspects of editing that a professional editor would tell you about. They are instead construction tips that help bring the text to life and add real interest and validity to the book. Some are also just common sense!

Once you have finished your first draft content accumulation stage you need to:

1. Read It Out Loud

2. Review It for Additional Material

3. Acknowledge References

4. Stay Focused on the Objective

5. Step Away From the Book

6. Edit Ruthlessly

7. Get Feedback and Edit Again

1. Read It Out Loud

Print out your manuscript. It's much easier to edit on paper than it is to edit on screen. I do feel guilty about printing the manuscript but I reduce the point size to the smallest I can read and print on fast economy to appease my conscience.

Seeing the printed document gives you a visual clue to how the page may look in a book. From that perspective you are not only looking for errors but the aesthetics on the page so you can ensure there is enough white space. This is therefore especially important at final proof stage when the book is designed and laid out.

This is an exciting time for a new author, so enjoy it. You will be able to see for the first time just how much you've done and have a physical product in your hand. I also find it reassuring to have a printed version in case something goes wrong with my computer. I had a nasty experience at university that involved working through the night and a power cut that has made me especially paranoid about such things!

It is very important that you read your manuscript out loud. Unless you're a professional editor you will not pick up nearly as many errors if you read it silently to yourself. Reading out loud means that errors become much easier to spot.

If you run out of breath in the middle of the sentence – it's too long. If you have to read the sentence three times to understand it – you need to simplify it. If you trip up or are confused by a sentence you know you have to rewrite it.

2. Review It for Additional Material

One of the additional advantages of reading your manuscript out loud is that as you read you are likely to be reminded of additional material or ideas that you could add that would strengthen the case.

If you are writing a book that stands as a testament to your ability to solve a number of particular business challenges, then you need to ensure that you have approached those challenges from as many angles as possible. That means that your book needs to be littered with examples, case studies, hypothetical examples, and wherever possible, verifiable third party research.

Not only does this add weight and credibility to your book but it makes the book more enjoyable to read.

Theory and ideas are always brought to life when they are accompanied by real life examples. It's always easier to understand something when we can see the idea or principle play out in a real world situation. It is therefore no longer an abstract notion but a living philosophy.

These additions also "speak" to different reading styles, which are important if you are to keep all your readers engaged. There are those that want human stories and examples and there are others that prefer cold hard facts. They want to know if there is theory and science behind your ideas.

For example, when I was writing this book I didn't know of any research that verified my opinion that writing a book was a powerful business development tool. As part of my research phase I found a fleeting mention to a possible study in another book. I went online to investigate and found that RainToday.com and Wellesley Hill Group had conducted a study into the exact topic I was writing about. Although it was done in 2006, it was still recent enough and specific enough to be of value. It wasn't a cheap study to buy at US$179, but I felt sure from my own experience that the findings would validate my argument. I sought written permission to quote from the survey and its addition adds independent evidence and has hopefully helped you realise just how important writing a book can be as a marketing and brand building exercise.

I make no secret of the fact that I'm a professional writer. It is therefore in my best interests to convince you of the merit of writing a book especially if in that process you realise you don't actually want to write the book yourself and hiring a ghostwriter may be the perfect solution. So it's fair to assume that you may believe my view is biased. What this study shows, however, is that it is not just my opinion. That independent verification is vital for building trust and establishing credibility.

If you think of anything you could add to your manuscript to strengthen the book, just make a note of it in the margin. Once you've been through your manuscript once, decide if it's relevant and adds to the merit of the argument or not. Don't add it straight away otherwise you may find you've already mentioned it elsewhere or you may find a more appropriate place for the idea.

3. Acknowledge References

I strongly believe that if you find an author or come across a study that you resonate with or like, then you are duty bound to reference that material properly. I remember receiving a call in late 2008 from a US motivational speaker who was interested in having me write a range of material for him including books, training programs and speeches. He wanted me to go to seminars and conferences and then synthesise the material into new product that he could sell. Apparently a friend of his, a very prominent sales trainer in the US, told him that there was nothing new left to say anyway and if you rewrite something three times it's yours! In other words, it was perfectly okay to steal other people's ideas and pass them off as your own.

I remember another instance when a would-be client approached me to write a book on networking. I asked him what he wanted to add to the topic and what new information he wanted to bring to the debate. He told me that he didn't have anything new and that all he really wanted me to do was buy a specific book which was apparently very good, read it and rewrite it to create a new product that he would then put his name to. Needless to say I didn't accept that commission.

I strongly disagree with this – if something is good enough to repeat, it's good enough to reference. Besides if we all really believed that there was nothing new to discover or nothing new to say or nothing new to invent then what a dreary world this would be. That's what Charles H. Duell, commissioner of the US Office of Patents, said in 1899, *"Everything that can be invented has been invented."* Clearly, he was wrong then and the idea is still wrong now.

If you realise that you don't really have anything new to say then either consider staying quiet or at the very least find an interesting or unusual way of saying it!

Think about sales books for example – everything that ever needed to be said about sales has been said. There really can't be much left to say in that particular industry. Yet there are always new sales books coming out because someone has found an interesting hook or unusual way of expressing the old information.

The key to writing a successful book is having something worthwhile to say. In my opinion, that doesn't mean simply regurgitating hundreds of other people's ideas and passing them off as your own, without any new input.

If you are using someone else's material then make absolutely sure you have their written, legal permission. And remember, unless all rights have been relinquished to previously created work the original author always owns moral rights.

4. Stay Focused on the Objective

Your book is going to be in the public domain for a long time. If it's online it could be there forever! So think about what you want the book to do for you and stay mindful of that objective as you edit. Avoid using examples or references that will date the book. That means don't write, "Recently I ..." or "within the past five years". Instead, date what you are talking about or add, "At the time of writing ...". That way the book still makes sense five or ten years from now. Remember, not everyone is going to read your book when you publish it. It will serve as a permanent marketing document for many years to come.

It may be that you want to drive your readers back to your website or Facebook page so that they register to join your online community where they can be informed of special offers or additional information products. Having bought the book, your reader may also now be eligible for a discount on your products or services.

For example, in the book *Natural Born Success* by Paul Burgess we directed people to the Link up International website. Paul's book was all about his proprietary psychometric testing tool, which gives people a real insight into what makes them tick. The information is invaluable in all aspects of life and this unique I.D. (Instinctive Drive) is established after completing a short questionnaire. Readers of the book were given a promotional code which gave them a discount on their I.D. Report.

What added value could you deliver to your readers so that you can direct them to your website and gather their contact details? Remember, if people go to the site to get your free report then they must consider it worthwhile based on the quality of your book, so the idea of keeping in touch with these people is common sense. Online material that delivers genuine assistance and value to your potential customers builds trust and allows you to develop a relationship. As long as you deliver on your promises and help them to achieve their goals then they will also, by default, help you to achieve yours.

5. Step Away From the Book

Part of the writing process is not writing. Once you have populated your Table of Contents framework and created your first draft manuscript, filled in the blanks, referenced everything properly, added any new material you've uncovered and ensured there are enough examples to bring the book to life, you need to put it aside and forget about it for at least a week.

Go and do something completely different. Don't peek. Don't fiddle. Don't add anything. Don't even think about it. If you suddenly think of a brilliant addition to make then just add it to your dedicated notebook and forget about it.

You need to have some space if you are to see your manuscript through cold eyes. It took me about 12 days to finish the first draft of this book and I was convinced I had almost nailed it. Yet after leaving it for a few days and getting a little distance from the material I could see how delusional that was! With perspective I was able to make some major improvements that I would not have seen had I immediately set about editing it.

Once you've left it to "cook" for a few days, go back and finish the editing process. That means reading it all again from scratch, preferably in one or two sittings. And always out loud!

6. Edit Ruthlessly

Once everything is in place, you need to edit ruthlessly. Writer William Faulkner said of the editing process, "Kill your darlings." And editing *is* every bit as torturous as that! It is so easy to become really attached to your writing and when it comes to editing you end up cutting a few words here and there.

It's not enough, you need to be ruthless. You need a cool head and cold heart – if it doesn't serve a purpose, remove it.

You will probably find some structural issues. On reading the book from start to finish you may decide that certain examples, stories or sections belong in a different place. You may also discover that you've repeated yourself too much or have used stories or examples more than once.

Have an open mind and make every word count. Or as William Strunk Jr, co-author of *The Elements of Style,* the famous little manual that has helped improve the writing of millions of its readers said, *"Vigorous writing is concise. A sentence should contain no unnecessary words, a paragraph no unnecessary sentences, for the same reason that a drawing should have no unnecessary lines and a machine no unnecessary parts. This requires not that the writer make all his sentences short, or that he avoid all detail and treat his subject only in outline, but that every word tell."*

Take time to find the right word. Don't overuse adjectives. Bring your writing to life with variety and cut out anything that is not adding to the message or delivering value to the reader.

It is always so much easier to edit ruthlessly if you find that you have written a great deal of content, 90,000 words+. That is why I recommend you add everything you can think of in the initial content creation stages.

If you find you only have 30,000 words or less it's hard to edit ruthlessly because you feel you have to hold on to every word in order to justify the book. If this is the case you may need to look at expanding sections that you had previously brushed over. Alternatively you could expand the context and include new sections or additional chapters.

7. Get Feedback and Edit Again

Once you've finished this second-round edit and you have your much-loved manuscript in your hot little hands, then it's preferable to get some feedback. Don't ever be tempted to seek that feedback after the first draft is complete. You'll only be embarrassed afterwards when you realise how much better it could have been with a proper edit.

I have to confess I didn't take my own advice when I originally wrote this book and it's a great reminder for me never to ignore good advice. I wrote the bulk of the first edition in November 2008. I was contracted to write another book in December and I really needed to get started if I was going to hit the deadline. I decided to send the first draft manuscript of this one to a couple of people so they could review it while I was busy with the *other* book. Only when I reviewed the book with more distance I was sorry I'd sent it out at all. I still received some really useful feedback but I was embarrassed at some of the errors in the first draft.

When you are ready for feedback, don't ask your friends and family – unless of course your friends and family happen to be experts in your industry or experts in writing or publishing. For example, one of my friends was very qualified to offer feedback as she is the marketing director for a global company. Her input really helped the finished product.

However, sometimes it's friends and family that can be the *least* enthusiastic and encouraging!

Remember, writing can be a very emotional and personal journey, and it is also a very subjective experience. You need to get constructive, informed feedback that will allow you to improve your manuscript. If you feel that you have friends and family members that can deliver that then by all means involve them, but be choosy about the people you share your book with.

There is no point, for example, sending it to a friend that thinks you are wonderful regardless of what you do and will never say anything other than gush about how fabulous it was. It might soothe your ego for a moment but it won't help you improve your book. You don't want to put people in an awkward position either, so regardless of where you send your manuscript, be sure to lay out the ground rules. That means telling people exactly what you're looking for:

- What did you like?

- What didn't work so well?

- Was anything unclear or confusing?

- How could I improve it?

- Do you think anything was missed?

- Do you think any section was over or under covered?

- Did you have any questions that were not answered?

- Did you find yourself wishing I'd covered anything or gone into more detail?

- Were there enough examples?

In addition, you need to gauge whether your friends and family are in a position to answer these questions or have sufficient experience in either your industry, business or in the process of writing a book to make helpful comments. If you had a friend who had been divorced four times you wouldn't ask him for relationship advice so don't ask people who know nothing about your industry or writing what they think of your book. They won't be able to help you.

Family and friends can also be notorious party poopers, so seek out someone in your industry that you trust and respect and ask *them* for some feedback. Constructive criticism at this stage can be critical so make sure they have your permission to give suggestions.

This stage can be nerve-racking. You need to be patient and not assume anything. If the people you ask are as busy as you are, it may take them a few weeks to get back to you. Their silence does not necessarily mean they hate it and just don't know how to tell you! Just get on with other things in the meantime.

When the verdict is in, try to detach yourself from the book and hear the suggestions with an open mind. You may get some great insights that really add to the value of the book. In the end, what you decide to take on board and what you decide to ignore is up to you – it's your book.

8. Get It Professionally Edited and Proofread

Once you've added whatever nuggets of gold that emerge from the review process, you are ready to have your book professionally edited and proof-read.

WRITER   VS   EDITOR

If your book is being published by a mainstream publisher then they will take care of this stage for you. If you are self-publishing, publishing online or using print-on-demand then you MUST have your manuscript professionally edited.

The editing process is usually a two-stage process. First, the editor will read it for accuracy, flow and consistency. Sometimes a writer can be so close to a subject that they assume a certain level of knowledge; the editor's job is to pick up areas where topics have not been adequately explained for the average reader. They will also make sure that cross-referencing is done properly and if you refer to something in chapter three that reference is actually in chapter three. They will be looking to make sure the book flows in a logical order and will also check the heading conventions. Most mainstream publishers of non-fiction will have three or four levels of headings. Each one will be given a different font and point size and those headings will help to guide the reader through the book. A good editor will also be looking out for consistency issues. For example, if you include percentages in your book the editor will make sure that they are all expressed the same way. There is often no right or wrong with editing – what makes it wrong is inconsistency. So if you write, "56%" on one page but "89 percent" on another and even "13 per cent" on another – that's wrong. And of course a good editor will tighten up your sentence structure and language where necessary. Their job is to tighten up the manuscript and polish it up. Think of a good editor as the difference between a Bronze medal at the Olympics and the Gold. There may only be a few hundredths of a second separating the athletes but that last hundredth of a second makes all the difference. It's the same with editing – you may not be able to tell what a good editor has actually done to your manuscript but it will just be better.

The second separate stage of the editing process is the proofreading, where the editor is only looking for spelling and grammar errors. Nothing screams "amateur" louder than a spelling mistake. Don't assume your word processing spell checker is enough – it's not. You should definitely use that resource but you need a human being to do the final check.

And that human being can't be you. Once you have written something and been immersed in it you stop seeing what is there and start to see what you think you wrote. Your brain no longer "reads", it "remembers". You need a pair of fresh professional eyes to ensure your manuscript is error-free. (I better make sure there isn't one in here after banging on about it so much!)

To illustrate this point, when I finished this book I made several passes to ensure it was in a good enough state to send to my editor. It's a bit like tidying the house before the cleaner arrives! I knew she would find some errors, of course, but was still surprised to find just how many. When I'm writing, the part of my brain that engages in spelling and grammar seems to turn off. One of my favourite and yet most embarrassing mistakes is "your" versus "you're". I know the grammatical difference and where each is appropriate and yet when I'm in the writing zone I don't see the error. Unfortunately, because I thought I wrote it correctly the first time, I often still don't see it at the editing stage because I'm reading what I think I wrote, not what is on the page. After all I *know* the difference so I'm not expecting to make the mistake but I still do. That sort of mistake can be extremely costly – especially for a writer. Don't run the risk – get a professional editor to review your manuscript.

It's also wise to repeat this proofreading process after the book has been designed and laid out. Even if something is right as it goes to the designer, little errors can sometimes creep in as the file is manipulated and converted into different software programs. If you want to be super sure it's 100 percent accurate, then proofread it again before it goes to press or is uploaded for print-on-demand.

You also have to decide where your main audience is and use spelling appropriate to that audience. For example, the main market for e-books is in the United States so you may want to use American English in your e-book. It's a personal choice. I prefer to write everything in the version of English I grew up with (UK English). If I mention currency I use the currency that is relevant to the story but I will also include a US$ equivalent to aid comprehension to a wider audience.

The All-Important Cover

If you want a traditional publishing deal and are successful in securing one then the publisher will handle the cover design. You will be involved in the process but they will take charge and use their expertise to decide the right approach.

If not, then you need to give it some thought as part of your overall strategy. The challenge is creating a cover appropriate for the sales channel while also appealing to your target market. If your book is bookshop bound then the cover is the most important real estate in your book. On the average, a bookstore browser will spend 8 seconds looking at the front cover and 15 seconds scanning the back cover. And considering this facility is now available in many online stores, where you can look more closely at the cover, contents and back cover, you need to get this right.

As discussed more and more people are searching for books online so it's also important to include keywords and phrases in the title and subtitle so that would-be readers can find you using a search engine. This is also true offline, although for different reasons. Online the subtitle is important because of what potential readers will search for using search engines. Stating the obvious can direct potential readers to your book. Offline, potential readers are still impatient, so if you have a clever title without a subtitle that succinctly explains the thrust of the book then it may be passed by for other competing titles that do.

If you are publishing online as well as aiming for a physical product try and marry the cover so it appeals to both online and offline audiences.

Bottom line – don't scrimp on design. If you are managing the process yourself, whether self-publishing, POD or e-book, make sure you hire a good designer because you really can tell a book by its cover. Having your book professionally designed and laid out can make a massive difference to sales and perhaps more importantly – credibility. Remember you are going to want to send this book to would-be clients so it needs to look fantastic.

Action Steps

Once you have populated your Table of Contents framework and created your first draft manuscript you need to start polishing.

1. Do you know of any research that would add weight to your proposition? If not, go online and look. If you do find a study that you think may be helpful then investigate it further. Remember to validate it offline wherever possible as the Internet isn't always the most reliable source of knowledge. It should only be viewed as a great starting place.

2. Do you need written permission to quote from a study, book or research paper? If you do, put that process in motion sooner rather than later. If you are quoting a sentence or short paragraph from a book then you probably don't need permission because of the "fair use" principle but you do need to reference that book. If you are unsure – check.

3. Consider what you could offer your readers to add extra value and drive them to your website or Facebook page. Do you have additional products, special offers or could you create helpful information products that would help your readers and build a marketing platform for you.

4. When it's time to read your book, go somewhere that you will not be disturbed and read the book out loud so you can hear how it sounds.

5. Shortlist a few people that you would consider showing your manuscript to and make contact. Tell them your plans and ask if they would be available to critique your book.

6. If you are publishing the book yourself source a good designer for the cover and internal layout.

7. If you are creating the physical book, work out how you are doing it before you start the design process so that your chosen designer works to the specifications of your printer and you don't waste money redoing work down the track.

8. Be prepared to read your book several times. If you are not thoroughly sick of it by the time it goes to press then you haven't read it enough times!

Summary of Key Points

- Getting the bulk of the content down onto paper is a huge piece of the puzzle. But the most important part is still to come.

- Turning the base content into a book requires attention to eight editing essentials so that you can apply the polish to your manuscript.

- Once you have finished your first draft content accumulation stage you need to read it out loud, review it for additional material, acknowledge references, stay focused on the objective, step away from the book, edit ruthlessly, get feedback and edit again.

- It is very important that you read your manuscript out loud. Reading out loud means that errors become much easier to spot.

- If you run out of breath in the middle of the sentence – it's too long. If you have to read the sentence three times to understand it – you need to simplify it. If you trip up or are confused by a sentence you know you have to rewrite it.

- One of the additional advantages of reading your manuscript out loud is that as you read you are likely to be reminded of additional material or ideas that you could add that would strengthen the case.

- If you think of anything you could add to your manuscript to strengthen the book, just make a note of it in the margin. Once you've been through your manuscript once, decide if it's relevant and adds to the merit of the argument or not.

- I strongly believe that if you find an author or come across a study that you resonate with or like then you are duty bound to reference that material properly.

- The key to writing a successful book is having something worthwhile to say. That doesn't mean simply regurgitating hundreds of other people's ideas and passing them off as your own, without any new input.

- Your book is going to be in the public domain for a long time. Think about what you want the book to do for you and stay mindful of that objective as you edit.

- It may be that you want to drive your readers back to your website or Facebook page so that they register to join your online community.

- Part of the writing process is not writing. Once you've created your first draft manuscript, you need to put it aside and forget about it for at least a week.

- Once you've left it to "cook" for a few days, go back and finish the editing process and edit ruthlessly.

- Take time to find the right word. Don't overuse adjectives. Bring your writing to life with variety and cut out anything that is not adding to the message or delivering value to the reader.

- When you are ready for feedback, don't ask your friends and family – unless of course your friends and family happen to be experts in your industry or experts in writing or publishing.

- Constructive criticism at this stage can be critical so make sure they have your permission to give suggestions.

- Once you've added whatever nuggets of gold that emerge from the review process, you are ready to have your book professionally edited and proofread.

- The editing process is usually a two-stage process. First, the editor will read it for accuracy, flow and consistency. The second separate stage of the editing process is the proofreading, where the editor is only looking for spelling and grammar errors.

- If you want a traditional publishing deal and are successful in securing one then the publisher will handle the cover design. If not, then you need to give it some thought as part of your overall strategy.

- Bottom line – don't scrimp on design. If you are managing the process yourself, whether self-publishing, POD or e-book, make sure you hire a good designer because you really can tell a book by its cover.

Chapter 12
Problems?

A problem clearly stated is a problem half solved.
~ Dorothea Brande

There are three major problems that I hear time and time again:

- Help! – I Hate Writing!

- Help! – Writing Hates Me!

- Help! – I Can't Find the Time!

Help! – I Hate Writing!

In the RainToday.com and Wellesley Hills Group study not everyone was enthusiastic about the merits of writing a book – 12 percent actually said, "It depends" and what it depended on was whether you enjoyed the writing process.

All too often, would-be writers start off with a romantic notion about life as a writer. It involves late nights, chain-smoking cigarettes and far too much black coffee or red wine. And yet the reality bears very little resemblance to the romance. It can be isolating and lonely. You may feel cut off from others as your mind churns over ideas and thoughts that no one else around you is likely to be remotely interested in!

Truth is, we may all be taught about the mechanics of writing, grammar, spelling and sentence structure but that doesn't automatically mean you will be naturally gifted at it or enjoy it.

I believe that we all have abilities and talents and the best use of our time and effort is to find out what those are and use them. Why torture yourself staring at a blank screen for hours when you could be using *your* unique talents and abilities to make more money, have more fun and do something you enjoy!

In some cases, the "author" simply doesn't want to write the book. I had one client approach me who had already written a successful book. It was obvious that he could write but it was a real struggle for him, he didn't enjoy the writing process. So he asked me to write his second one for him.

Help! – Writing Hates Me!

Some would-be authors start writing their book and then part way through, they hit the wall. They either stop writing or become disheartened because what they have created turns out to be nowhere near as good as they envisaged. The translation from their mind to the page is clunky and disappointing. The writer realises their much dreamt of book is actually not very good and doesn't do justice to their ideas and theories.

Sometimes a writer keeps writing and writing and writing and has a vast amount of information but no structure or order to it. As a result the material loses impact and becomes turgid and uninteresting. Sometimes the book becomes too long, other times it's too short – either way the "author" recognises that perhaps writing isn't their forte and they should seek some assistance.

The great news for these people is that if you have gathered together a great deal of the content, then the process for a ghostwriter can be relatively swift and you can have your much dreamt of book fairly quickly.

In the end if depends on the quality of the content created, as more information doesn't always equate to a quick-fix. Starting with a blank canvas can sometimes be a whole lot easier.

Help! – I Can't Find the Time!

Many would-be authors are busy professionals, speakers, consultants or business owners and despite recognising the value of writing their own book, simply can't find the time from their already packed schedule.

They fully appreciate that writing a book offers a unique opportunity to secure their position in their industry and capitalise on the intellectual property within their business. More often than not, they already see how they could create additional knowledge-based revenue streams but it's a distant dream. They usually realise that if they don't write their book there is a very good chance someone else will and their position as leader in their field will be usurped. Like Charles Darwin, it is this realisation that spurs them to action. They decide either to write the book themselves – or to hire a ghostwriter.

When I meet these people they are usually extremely frustrated. Often they have no shortage of ideas but a severe shortage of time. They also have a great desire to write their book, but it has become a burden that weighs heavily upon them.

If years have passed and all you have are some scattered scribbles on napkins and the back of airline boarding passes, if you are sick of staring at a blank screen, or you've written something and you don't like it, or if you simply don't have the time, I suggest you stop beating yourself up about it and do what all the great business leaders and entrepreneurs have done – outsource. Perhaps it's time for a new approach. Perhaps it's time to hire a ghostwriter.

Summary of Key Points

- There are three major problems that I hear time and time again, Help! – I Hate Writing, Help! – Writing Hates Me, and Help! – I Can't Find the Time!

- We may all be taught about the mechanics of writing, grammar, spelling and sentence structure but that doesn't automatically mean you will be naturally gifted at it or enjoy it.

- Why torture yourself staring at a blank screen for hours when you could be using *your* unique talents and abilities to make more money, have more fun and do something you enjoy!

- Some would-be authors start writing their book and then part way through, they hit the wall. They either stop writing or become disheartened because what they have created turns out to be nowhere near as good as they envisaged.

- Sometimes the book becomes too long, other times it's too short – either way the "author" recognises that perhaps writing isn't their forte and they should seek some assistance.

- Many would-be authors are busy professionals, speakers, consultants or business owners and despite recognising the value of writing their own book, simply can't find the time from their already packed schedule.

- If, so far, your efforts have not delivered the book you want then I suggest you stop beating yourself up about it and hire a ghostwriter.

Chapter 13

Hire a Ghostwriter

I perceived that to express those impressions, to write that essential book, which is the only true one, a great writer does not, in the current meaning of the word, invent it, but, since it exists already in each one of us, interprets it. The duty and the task of a writer are those of an interpreter.
~ Marcel Proust

If you desperately want to write the book and writing every word yourself is genuinely important to you, then there is no other way than to dedicate time to it and make that task a priority.

If, however, you just want your book written and published then perhaps you should consider hiring a ghostwriter. For a long time ghostwriters were as elusive as their title suggested. Publishers didn't talk about them and they lived quite happily in the shadows. Today "authors" and publishers alike recognise the advantages of having a ghostwriter involved in a project.

When people learn that I'm a ghostwriter, it always causes a stir. Some people have never heard of a ghostwriter and are often confused by the concept. The inevitable question surely follows as night follows day, "But doesn't it bother you that someone else gets the credit for your work?"

But true ghostwriting is not like that. As a ghostwriter I am just a conduit for the knowledge and expertise that the client already has. I am not creating the content out of thin air. Instead I gather it from the client, adding some additional research where necessary. I then create a viable structure and weave all the information together to create the finished manuscript. As such, the book is still very much the client's book – it is their skill, knowledge and expertise that's contained in the book, not mine.

As a ghostwriter I offer a bridge between the "author's" mind and the written page. My job therefore is to interview and extract the content required to write that book and then organise it in a way so that the author not only recognises his or her own thoughts but also their personality too. The whole idea of ghostwriting is to bring my expertise together with some other form of expertise – be that marketing, building straw bale houses or Internet publishing.

I am occasionally asked to write books from a list of bullet points, but this is not ghostwriting and I don't accept those types of commissions. To me ghostwriting is helping someone else to write a book that I could not write without their input. If a client is an expert in a particular field then they are qualified to write that book, I'm not. My role is to extract their knowledge and order it in such a way as to create an engaging book that showcases their expertise.

Although it's a strange analogy, ghostwriters are like surrogate mothers. They may carry the book during the gestation period, growing and developing the book through to completion but the "genetic material" that creates the book belongs to the client. As such, once the book is out in the world it is very much the client's book. The ghostwriter disappears from the process and the client becomes the author. Hiring a ghostwriter is not cheating! It is a legitimate and efficient way to achieve your desired outcome when you can't or don't want to write it yourself.

I love writing and consider myself truly fortunate to have discovered my passion in life, and the ability to use my inherent skills. I am also very grateful that I have been able to make a good living from writing – a profession notoriously poorly paid. But writing can be lonely sometimes and ghostwriting offers a balance. Not only do I get to meet interesting people but I get to help them fulfil a lifelong dream. I thoroughly enjoy learning new subjects and there can't be many professions in the world where you get paid to learn a new subject. Over the years I've learned about topics as diverse as mind/body medicine, alternative therapies, stock market investing, property investing, business coaching and psychology, personality profiling, property renovation and Neuro Linguistic Programming (NLP).

How Does Ghostwriting Work?

There is no "ghostwriter's rulebook", so how you work with your chosen writer is a matter of negotiation. Not all ghostwriters are the same. Some will offer structural advice and ideas for improvement, some won't. Some will assist with creative ideas and suggestions for chapter titles and style and others won't. Some will be happy to research and source additional content, others won't. Some will expect you to provide the bulk of the content, either verbally or in writing, others will be happy to interview you.

The type of writer you need depends on you. If you have a very clear idea of what you want and can give the writer a detailed brief, then you could get away with a less hands-on writer. If your thinking is still fairly fluid, and you are not necessarily clear about how the book will finish up and prefer to see it evolve – then you need a more experienced writer.

You also need to consider your own personal style and communication preference. For example, do you want to work face-to-face or are phone calls and email easier? In theory, it doesn't matter where the writer is physically located because of Internet access, email and communication technology such as Skype. However, it is best to hire someone whose first language is the language you speak and also, if possible, someone who understands the nuances of your country. For example, my first language is English and I have clients in the UK, Australia, US and Canada where cultures are fairly similar and the language only needs slight modifications. There is no need to meet your writer face-to-face, although some authors prefer that connection. In truth, I do, but it's not always possible. The main thing is that you find a writer that understands you and your culture.

Sourcing the right writer for your project will also depend on what you already have. In my experience would-be authors either have:

- A rough manuscript

- An idea but no written material

- A rough idea and additional material from other sources

If you have already laboured over your book and therefore already have a lot of written material then chances are you have already done a lot of thinking about the topic. If you already have a rough manuscript then you may only need a professional editor. If, however, you are not happy with what you've created you may need the help of a ghostwriter who can provide a better structure and pull everything together in a more cohesive and polished manner.

If you only have an idea but no written material then you will almost certainly need a more experienced ghostwriter. The idea is certainly critical but it is not enough. However, if you have a vast amount of information in your head and have business examples and case studies that spring to mind as soon as someone asks you the right question, then creating a book would be relatively straightforward.

In this case the writer will usually schedule a series of interviews where he or she will ask questions to elicit the information they require. Most writers will provide those questions ahead of time so the client can make sure they are fully prepared and can mull over some of the more in-depth questions. The interviews will be recorded, transcribed and that information will then form the basis for the content.

For some authors they just want a book to complement their business or speaking engagements and whilst they don't have anything in writing they may have DVDs or audio recordings of their presentations. They may also have old material that needs to be updated or woven into the book.

The writer can then use those other sources of information to create a book. For example, I wrote a book for John Wiley's & Sons and Channel 7 in Australia to complement their successful TV show *Auction Squad*. All I was given were some recordings of the shows. I visited the production one day and met the various hosts but that was it. I then watched the shows, researched new material where I needed it and wrote the book in six weeks.

The exact nature of your ghostwriting project depends on how both parties want to set it up. It usually involves several meetings either over the phone or in person, followed by phone calls and email exchanges.

Advantages of Hiring a Ghostwriter

When you accept that not everyone is a natural writer then you can more clearly see the advantages of hiring a ghostwriter to help you create your book. The key benefits of hiring an experienced ghostwriter are:

- Structure

- Content

- Speed

- Leverage

- Assessment

- Contacts

Structure

Finding an appropriate structure for your book is one of the hardest tasks in writing. It's obvious when it's wrong and yet remains completely invisible when it's right. Having the knowledge in your head is one thing, finding a way to express that knowledge in a meaningful and interesting way is quite another.

An effective ghostwriter will be able to immerse themselves in your content and emerge with a range of possible structure suggestions including Table of Contents and chapter headings. They may also make some suggestions on a hook that would interest mainstream publishers and generate sales.

Finding the patterns in the chaos is an underestimated yet critical skill of a good ghostwriter. It is often lack of structure that leads would-be authors to a ghostwriter in the first place. Without an idea of how to order the information authors drown in their own content and become overwhelmed by the sheer volume of information they want to get across. Without the framework they get stuck and usually stop writing.

Content

Two heads are always better than one. If you hire a collaborative ghostwriter he or she will usually be very widely read and will often have ideas and knowledge that can strengthen your argument and add to your manuscript. Having an impartial, objective and collaborative mind involved in writing your book can throw up all sorts of fortuitous surprises.

When your chosen ghostwriter is from outside your industry he or she will look at your book from different angles. This altered perspective will always improve the manuscript because it can draw in existing research and studies from other fields that are not only relevant to your book but also add interest and flavour.

A collaborative ghostwriter will usually suggest additional content and then it's up to you whether you want to accept that content or not. The book remains *your* book but you may get some interesting little snippets along the way. For example, I wrote a book for a business and marketing consultant, trainer and speaker in Australia who specialises in helping business owners make more money while working less hours. The last part of the book was dedicated to practical strategies that business owners could easily implement for immediate results. But once I wrote this section it didn't feel right. It was too disconnected. There was no context or hook that tied everything together. The book was about taking immediate and fast action to make more money for the readers' businesses, and so I suggested that we rework the practical element of the book around an acronym – Financial, Acceleration, Success, Techniques (F.A.$.T.). My client loved it and I wrote 21 separate chapters describing these techniques.

One of the more interesting elements of my writing career is my experience of cumulative knowledge. Every book I write leads me into a subject area that I didn't previously know about and yet, without fail, every subsequent book I've written, regardless of the topic, has been able to benefit from that new knowledge. I'm able to draw in examples, studies and ideas that add variety and depth to the writing, even if it is in an entirely different field to anything I have written about before.

Speed

When you are doing something for the first time – be that rollerblading, surfing or writing a book – there is always an element of trial and error. And that takes time.

Hiring a ghostwriter to help you flesh out your ideas, structure your book and write it can save you months or even years of torture. Depending on the length and complexity of the material discussed in the book, an experienced ghostwriter should be able to write your book in six to eight weeks. Memoirs or biographies can take significantly longer.

Obviously how quickly a book can be finished is not just down to the skill and speed of the ghostwriter. If you hire a ghostwriter you must recognise your role in the process and provide the necessary interview time and set time aside to edit the book. Hiring a ghostwriter will definitely speed up the delivery of your manuscript but it is not a hands-off process. The writer – regardless of how good or experienced – can't write the book without you. They are not able to stick a USB stick behind your ear and download everything in your head so communication is paramount. The writer will need access and you will have to provide timely and accurate feedback so that the finished manuscript reflects your wishes.

If you are committed and provide the necessary access and review time then you will be astonished at how quickly your book can come together.

Leverage

Hiring a ghostwriter allows you to leverage your time and effort. If you are struggling to write, or hate writing, then there is an opportunity cost associated with that wasted time. Not only do you avoid the mental anguish and stress caused by trying to force yourself to write but there are financial implications too. According to BookStatistics.com it takes an average of 725 hours to write a non-fiction title. So before you rush off to write your own book at the expense of your business or practice you might want to multiply 725 by your hourly rate and see how much it will *really* cost you to write your own book.

Instead, you can maintain your billable hours and do what *you* do best, and hire a ghostwriter to do what *they* do best. Not only will you probably get a better product, you'll enjoy the process more and probably come out ahead financially! Ghostwriters are writing all the time, and as such, their expertise allows them to create a polished manuscript much quicker than someone who is writing a book for the first time.

Assessment

This book is written from the assumption that you want to write a non-fiction book to develop your business and take your career and income to new heights. It is also assumed that you want to impart some knowledge and help readers to gain insight and knowledge in your area of expertise.

There is a learning model which is often used in training called the conscious competence learning matrix. The origins of this matrix are unknown although sources as old as Confucius and Socrates are cited as possible originators. The four stages of the model refer to:

- Unconscious incompetence

- Conscious incompetence

- Conscious competence

- Unconscious competence

When we are learning a new subject, we start off unconsciously incompetent (I don't know I don't know); we move to conscious incompetence (I know I don't know); through to conscious competence where we have learned the new skill (I know I know); until finally it becomes second nature and you become unconsciously competent (I don't know I know).

The essence of the idea is that when we are really good at something we become unconsciously competent, meaning we stop thinking about how it is we know how to do something. When you start driving a car, for example, you don't know about the clutch and how it must be eased out gently so you end up stalling the car or kangaroo-hopping along the road. Soon you realise you need to find out what you don't know, so you take lessons. At first you are nervous and are very conscious of looking in the mirrors and doing everything in the correct sequence. Once you've been driving for a while it becomes unconscious and you are no longer consciously aware of checking mirrors etc. – you just drive. You are unconsciously competent.

If you are writing a book about a particular subject, chances are you are unconsciously competent regarding your subject matter. To be honest, if you're not then you probably shouldn't be writing a book on the subject! The challenge with your expertise, however, is that you may gloss over subjects and miss the little nuances of detail that are necessary for the accurate transference of knowledge. Crucial pieces of information might be missing, because you have assumed that the reader has greater or deeper knowledge than they actually have. For example, I could have assumed that you had already come across the conscious competence learning matrix because it is so prevalent in corporate training. But you may not have come in contact with it and without some explanation this section would be meaningless to you.

Once a reader stops understanding or is confused, then you run the risk of losing them and your opportunity to assist the reader is lost.

Hiring a ghostwriter who may not be an expert in your field means that you have an assessment and comprehension check built into the writing process. If your ghostwriter can't understand what you're talking about then you need to clarify your explanation until they do. You have to find a balance between going over old ground for some more knowledgeable readers and confusing others. And remember, confusion will lose you readers. Having someone involved in the process to question you and force you to explain in sufficient detail can dramatically improve understanding, which can widen your audience and create a much more powerful book.

This questioning process can also be very revealing as you realise just how knowledgeable you are on your subject.

Contacts

If you use an experienced ghostwriter, then chances are they will have contacts in the publishing world. If you want to secure a mainstream publishing contract then those contacts are priceless and can mean the difference between success and failure.

As you will discover in the next section of this book there are now many ways to publish your book but if you still want a traditional publisher then just getting your manuscript looked at can be a challenge. If your ghostwriter has established links and has a proven track record with existing large publishers then you will significantly improve your chances of securing a publishing contact.

For example, I have been commissioned many times by John Wiley & Sons and have developed a relationship with several of the commissioning editors over many years. As a result should a client want a publishing contract with that publisher I can at least ensure the manuscript gets reviewed because they know what quality to expect. No ghostwriter can guarantee publication, but they can open doors and that can make all the difference.

Most experienced ghostwriters will also know and use professional editors, proofreaders, indexers, designers and print-on-demand experts who can assist after the manuscript is written.

Disadvantages of Hiring a Ghostwriter

Hiring a ghostwriter is not all peaches and cream; there are drawbacks. The main disadvantages of this approach are:

- Cost

- Ownership

Cost

Obviously the main disadvantage is that you have to pay the ghostwriter. How much depends on the writer and how much quality content you have – either in writing or in your head.

It is often procrastination and concern about the cost that causes clients to postpone hiring a ghostwriter. Often would-be authors resent the idea of paying someone else to do something they *could* theoretically do themselves. But knowing you could write a book, or even that you want to write a book, unfortunately doesn't mean you will end up writing one.

In addition, if you add up the cost of wasted billable hours, or the cost of alternative marketing activity such as a direct marketing campaign, or a print advertising campaign, then hiring a ghostwriter to create a book you're really proud of is actually extremely cost-effective. Remember, the key statistics from The RainToday.com and Wellesley Hill Group study:

- 96 percent reported that their book generated more clients.

- 94 percent reported that their book generated more leads.

- 87 percent reported that their book allowed them to charge higher fees.

- 87 percent reported that their book allowed them to generate a more desirable client base.

- 76 percent reported that their book allowed them to close more deals.

What other marketing strategy do you know that can deliver those results? And remember, every year you waste putting it off is another year you lose these potential benefits.

Ownership

If you hire someone else to write your book, you may feel a little removed from the final product and may not therefore feel the same sense of ownership and accomplishment when the book is finished. However, as long as you find a writer that is collaborative and is willing to take the time to reflect your style and personality then you will still read yourself in the pages and feel as though it truly is *your* book. Plus if you find the right person you will know that the finished product does justice to your ideas and you have a product that both parties are proud of.

If, however, the physical writing process is very important to you, then hiring a ghost may not be the answer. If you want to be able to say, "I wrote this book" and mean it, then employing someone else to do it for you will not feel right. It may end up robbing you of the sense of ownership and pride you seek in having written it yourself.

If that's the case then you just have to go back to the start of the book and follow the process and make it a priority.

Hiring A Ghostwriter Might Suit You If:

- You hate writing.

- You love writing but don't have the time.

- You want a book quickly but have no way of dedicating the time to write it.

- You are happy to pay for what you want.

- You don't enjoy working alone.

- You don't have the ability to create the book you want.

- You're fed up of writing "write my book" on your annual "To Do" list.

Cost of Hiring a Ghostwriter

How much you can expect to pay depends on the ghostwriter, his or her experience, whether that person has publishing contacts and also whether or not they are prepared to share revenue or want a straight payment.

Allowing for inflation, the RainToday.com and Wellesley Hill Group study specified that the mean cost of hiring a ghostwriter was US$23,000 (£15,000). In some cases the ghostwriter also received between 15 – 20 percent of author royalties. Obviously the final cost depends on the length of your book and how clear you are about what you want but this is a good ballpark indication.

You *can* find writers on websites such as Guru.com or Elance.com who will charge considerably less than that, but most people using these sites expect to pay a ghostwriter very little and like everything in life you get what you pay for.

If you do want to try to find a writer this way then you will need to register and then post your project and writers will bid on the work. Make sure you give as much information as you can so that the writer knows what they are bidding on. Include the subject matter, whether you have anything already written, how long you want the book to be and how much you are willing to pay. Don't put the most you are willing to pay but don't put the lowest either otherwise you will not attract the right writer. Always check the writer's own website as well as their Guru or Elance profile and ask for samples or examples of previous work and check references if possible.

I am constantly shocked at how little people are willing to pay to have their book written and yet they will assure would-be writers that the project is easy. Writing a book is not easy and it requires time, skill and patience – besides if it really was that easy then surely they would write it themselves. Guru and Elance are best suited to people who are seeking to create a product. Often it doesn't really matter how good that product is as long as the marketing is slick and they sell it in enough numbers. By the time the reader realises that the book isn't worth the paper it's printed on, the money is in the bank. If you are seeking to create your legacy book that cements your position in your industry and acts as a business development tool then it really is worth paying a little more to secure an experienced writer with a proven track record.

Remember, your book will act as an exclusive business card so it's worth paying for quality. You wouldn't expect to pay peanuts for a professional marketing campaign so why would you expect to pay peanuts for a professionally created book which acts as a permanent marketing campaign?

This is your brand document; it details your vision, brand values and how you can help clients. It's your reputation in print and it has the power to transform your business. Sourcing the cheapest writer you can find is often a false economy and could potentially damage your brand and reputation.

When it comes to money, some ghostwriters prefer to keep it simple and charge a fee, others prefer a smaller fee and part revenue and others are willing to take a risk and plump for revenue. Revenue-based agreements are, however, rare in the business non-fiction sector – unless you have a natural market and can guarantee a receptive audience. If you are keen to find a writer who is willing to take a gamble with your project and doesn't want any up-front payment, expect to split your revenue 50/50. Remember, without the writer the chance of bringing your project to fruition is limited – 50 percent of something is better than 100 percent of nothing.

Most writers will require payment up-front. Expect to pay half the expected invoice before the project starts and the final payment on receipt of the finished and accepted manuscript.

Where Could I Find a Ghostwriter?

If you are searching for a ghostwriter then contact me through my website – www.wordarchitect.com. Have a ferret around the site and have a look at the books I've written and the feedback and comments I've received from happy clients. If you feel I might be the right person then get in touch and let's talk about your project.

On the other hand, if you don't think I'm the right fit for what you need, there are a number of online freelance sites such as Elance.com and Guru. com. Guru, for example, is a large freelance marketplace that allows individuals to post their requirements across a wide range of sectors including writing. You just wait for writers to bid for the job and decide who you want to hire. I used Guru.com to find a cartoonist to create the various cartoons I've included in this book.

Try and give as much information as you can so that prospective writers can provide a meaningful pitch. Don't forget to include a payment range. I wouldn't quote the highest amount you are prepared to pay for the job but at the same time make it clear that you don't expect to pay next to nothing, otherwise you will not get the calibre of writer that you should be looking for.

When assessing your would-be writer it's always better if you like the person. This isn't someone who is going to knock up a brochure for you. It's someone that you could potentially be spending a fair bit of time with – even if it's just over the phone.

Talk to the writer and have a chat about your expectations and what it is you are trying to achieve. See if you resonate with that person or not and try and find someone that is on your wavelength.

Ask for references and follow them up. Ask to see examples of their work, preferably ones you can verify. For example, I can tell you the books I've written and I can't have made it up because I am mentioned in the "Acknowledgements" section of those books. That's verified. If someone can't verify their involvement in something or doesn't have past work to show you, it doesn't mean they can't do the job. But they should be willing to provide you with some sample chapters without obligation so you can see for yourself whether they can actually write – before you part with any money.

Everyone has to start somewhere. When I started writing books I didn't have a portfolio of work I could provide but I was willing to remove all the risk for the client so that they didn't pay anything until they could see for themselves that I could write their book.

Even after 35 plus books I still guarantee my work in this way. Although I'm confident I can write the book, before I was a writer I was a marketer and risk reversal is a powerful tool to help people "take the plunge". I appreciate that writing a book is a big commitment; it's not something people want to get wrong! So by removing the risk the client can be assured that they can make an accurate choice based on their specific needs. I write a chapter of their book and then if they like it we start the project, and if they don't they walk away without any obligation. To date, everyone I've written sample chapters for has decided to employ me as their ghost.

Remember, good writing is subjective so you may be referred to a writer that your friend thinks is great but you don't – it's just a matter of finding a writer that fits with your style and personality so that the process is enjoyable and productive.

Most people I've met over the years, from taxi drivers to multimillionaire entrepreneurs and CEOs, have expressed a desire to write a book – yet only a small handful of them ever do. A good ghostwriter can help to ensure that your book doesn't go unwritten. If writing a book is important to you and you are no further forward than you were three years ago then perhaps it's time to hire a ghostwriter.

What Will I Need to Do?

Just because you decide to hire a ghostwriter doesn't mean you abdicate all responsibility. You need to mutually agree a timeline and both parties need to stick to that timeline. You also need to be available at scheduled times for telephone meetings and interviews. And by available I don't mean "in between meetings" or while you've nipped out for the shopping. This is important work which deserves mutual respect. The ghostwriter may prepare questions in advance so you need to be ready to answer those questions in a quiet uninterrupted session.

If you want your book to be a true reflection of what you believe, you have to tell your writer what that is. Give them as much information as possible including background material or company information so they can get a fuller picture of your business. If this makes you nervous then ask your writer to sign a confidentiality or non-disclosure agreement prior to providing any information.

Once the book is written and together you have filled in the gaps and answered all the queries, you need to read and review the book. And that doesn't mean you read it at the airport lounge or on the train or while you're waiting for the kettle to boil. You need to schedule blocks of time where you can properly engage with the material. You need to run through the same editing process outlined in Chapter 11. That means thinking about where you can add more stories or testimonials. Does any external evidence, or science, research or theories, spring to mind when you read a passage? If they do, make a note and ask your writer to find the source, or if you know where that source is, point them in the right direction.

You also have to ensure that what is said is accurate – you are liable for the accuracy of your book, not the ghostwriter. If you tell your writer facts and figures about your business it's your responsibility to ensure they are correct.

Manage Expectations

The key to any productive working relationship is to manage expectations. Both parties need to be clear regarding what is expected of them. You should work out a timeline with relevant milestones firmly in place. You need to know what you can reasonably expect from your writer and the writer needs to know what they can expect from you, bearing in mind that you probably have a thriving business to run.

Think about the worst-case scenario and discuss these options with your writer. For example, what happens if you decide to cancel in the middle of the project? Also you need to discuss how the writer will be acknowledged so there is no miscommunication. Some people want the ghostwriter to be as invisible as their job title would suggest. Others are happy to thank the writer for their assistance in the "Acknowledgements" section. It's best to discuss your preference up-front and remember it works both ways. For example, I once had a client who wanted me to be anonymous unless I became a famous writer in my own right in which case he would be able to advertise that I wrote his book! Needless to say, that clause was removed. You can't have your cake and eat it.

The simplest way to manage expectations is by having your writer sign a mutually-agreed contract. How complicated this becomes is up to you but to protect both parties it should cover, at a minimum:

- The legal nature of the working relationship. This should also include whether the writer will be acknowledged and, if so, how.

- An overview of the financial terms, including dates for payment and what happens in a dispute.

- An overview of the timing agreements. What each party agrees to do and what happens if one or other party doesn't meet those terms. For example, if you want the book written in six weeks but don't give the writer access to information or interview time then you can't really expect that deadline to be met.

- A description of services and clarification of any potential conflicts of interest.

- A description of any research required and who is responsible for it.

- A disclaimer of liability for accuracy of information. The writer is not liable to verify anything the business owner tells him or her is true.

- Details of how many revisions are accounted for in the price. Usually there will be one or two rounds of revisions. Be aware, however, if you decide to change the focus of the book halfway through, you will incur additional costs.

- Any agreements with the writer to use their contacts, but acknowledging that this is no guarantee of publication.

- Under what circumstances a refund would be considered.

- Ownership of rights and authorship.

- Confidentiality agreement and ownership of all materials.

- Details regarding termination by death, disability, or written notice.

- Details of legal written notice, severability, arbitration, and location for legal disputes.

If you want a book but don't have the time, inclination or ability to write it then hiring a ghostwriter may be the perfect solution.

Summary of Key Points

- If you desperately want to write the book and writing every word yourself is genuinely important to you, then there is no other way than to dedicate time to it and make that task a priority.

- If, however, you just want your book written and published then perhaps you should consider hiring a ghostwriter.

- Today "authors" and publishers alike recognise the advantages of having a ghostwriter involved in a project.

- A ghostwriter is a conduit for the knowledge and expertise that the client already has. As such, the book is still very much the client's book – it is their skill, knowledge and expertise that's contained in the book, not the ghostwriter's.

- There is no "ghostwriter's rulebook", so how you work with your chosen writer is a matter of negotiation. Not all ghostwriters are the same.

- If you have a very clear idea of what you want and can give the writer a detailed brief, then you could get away with a less hands-on writer. If your thinking is still fairly fluid, and you are not necessarily clear about how the book will finish up and prefer to see it evolve – then you need a more experienced writer.

- Sourcing the right writer for your project will also depend on what you already have. Most would-be authors either have a rough manuscript, an idea but no written material, or a rough idea and additional material from other sources.

- The key benefits of hiring an experienced ghostwriter are structure, content, speed, leverage, assessment, contacts.

- An effective ghostwriter will be able to immerse themselves in your content and emerge with a range of possible structure suggestions including Table of Contents and chapter headings.

- Two heads are always better than one. If you hire a collaborative ghostwriter he or she will usually be very widely read and will often have ideas and knowledge that can strengthen your argument and add to your manuscript.

- Hiring a ghostwriter to help you flesh out your ideas, structure your book and write it can save you months or even years of torture.

- Depending on the length and complexity of the material discussed in the book, an experienced ghostwriter should be able to write your book in six to eight weeks. Memoirs or biographies can take significantly longer.

- Hiring a ghostwriter allows you to leverage your time and effort.

- According to BookStatistics.com it takes an average of 725 hours to write a non-fiction title. So before you rush off to write your own book you might want to multiply 725 by your hourly rate and see how much it will *really* cost you to write your own book.

- Instead you can maintain your billable hours and do what *you* do best, and hire a ghostwriter to do what *they* do best.

- If you are writing a book about a particular subject, chances are you are unconsciously competent regarding your subject matter. The challenge with your expertise, however, is that you may gloss over subjects and miss the little nuances of detail that are necessary for the accurate transference of knowledge.

- Hiring a ghostwriter who may not be an expert in your field means that you have an assessment and comprehension check built into the writing process.

- If you use an experienced ghostwriter, then chances are they will have contacts in the publishing world.

- Most experienced ghostwriters will also know and use professional editors, proofreaders, indexers, designers and print-on-demand experts who can assist after the manuscript is written.

- Hiring a ghostwriter is not all peaches and cream; there are drawbacks. The main disadvantages of this approach are cost and ownership.

- Obviously the main disadvantage is that you have to pay the ghostwriter. How much depends on the writer and how much quality content you have – either in writing or in your head.

- If you hire someone else to write your book, you may feel a little removed from the final product and may not therefore feel the same sense of ownership and accomplishment when the book is finished.

- Hiring a ghostwriter may suit you if you hate writing, love writing but don't have the time, want a book quickly, are happy to pay for what you want, don't enjoy working alone, don't have the ability to create the book you want, or you are fed up of writing "write my book" on your annual "To Do" list.

- Allowing for inflation, the RainToday.com and Wellesley Hill Group study specified that the mean cost of hiring a ghostwriter was US$23,000 (£15,000). In some cases the ghostwriter also received between 15 – 20 percent of author royalties.

- You can find writers on websites such as Guru.com or Elance.com who will charge considerably less than that, but like everything in life you get what you pay for.

- Remember, your book will act as an exclusive business card so it's worth paying for quality.

- If you are searching for a ghostwriter then contact me through my website www.wordarchitect.com.

- Alternatively, you could post your project on websites such as Guru. com or Elance.com.

- Talk to the writer and see if you resonate with that person and try and find someone that is on your wavelength. Ask for references and follow them up. Ask to see examples of their work, preferably ones you can verify.

- Just because you decide to hire a ghostwriter doesn't mean you abdicate all responsibility. You need to mutually agree a timeline and both parties need to stick to that timeline.

- Once the book is written and together you have filled in the gaps and answered all the queries, you need to read and review the book.

- The key to any productive working relationship is to manage expectations. Both parties need to be clear regarding what is expected of them.

- If you want a book but don't have the time, inclination or ability to write it then hiring a ghostwriter may be the perfect solution.

PART THREE

WHAT ARE THE PUBLISHING OPTIONS?

Writing a book is only part of the puzzle. Once you have your finished manuscript you still need to get it published. The old way, and indeed the only way, that an author used to be able to see their book in print was if they could convince a traditional publisher to get involved. That is no longer the case. Today you can seek a mainstream publisher or you can choose to self-publish or use print-on-demand technology, or you can publish your book electronically.

Part three explores all the options available to you and their relative advantages and disadvantages so you can ascertain what is best for you. It's important to be aware of these differences because the processes that you need to follow differ depending on what you choose.

Chapter 14
The Old Way – Traditional Publishing

To write what is worth publishing, to find honest
people to publish it, and get sensible people to read
it, are the three great difficulties in being an author.
~ Charles Caleb Colton

In the past the only way you could be published was by convincing a publisher of the merits of your book. As a result, the balance of power was very much weighted in favour of the publishers rather than the writers. The publishers remained in their ivory towers and hundreds of thousands clamoured for their attention every year. Traditional publishing today is still inundated with unsolicited manuscripts that form Paper Mountains known as the "slush pile".

With the best will in the world, publishers would never be able to read everything that is sent to them. Consequently, the chances of your manuscript being picked up by a publisher from an unsolicited approach is about as likely as you winning €100 million in the Euro lottery – all to yourself!

The bottom line is this... to automatically assume that some big publisher will snap up your manuscript with verve and passion and you'll make millions in royalty income is pure fiction. Sorry! But I'm a great believer in honesty and managing expectations. Literary success is on the whole limited to the publishers, not the authors. It is an incredibly one-sided and antiquated industry and the more you know about the reality of that the better placed you are to find a publishing strategy that works for you.

Fame and fortune for authors is rare – very, very rare. It could happen to you and I hope it does but the probability is extremely low. There is definitely still money to be made by being an author but usually only if you view your book as an exclusive business card and use it as a springboard to increased sales and profile.

Advantages of Traditional Publishing

There are several advantages of having your book published by a large well-known traditional publisher, but the most significant are:

- Credibility

- Production

- Marketing

Credibility

Credibility is the main advantage touted by traditional publishing. According to the publishing industry a book published with them has more credibility and kudos than a book which is self-published. The logic of this assumption is sound in that anyone can self-publish and there is no quality control or assessment involved whereas not everyone can secure a publishing contract with a mainstream publisher.

The reality, however, is a little different. For a start mainstream publishers don't really assess on quality they assess on saleability. Any cursory look around the supermarket bookshelves or airport bookshop will confirm that traditional publishers are primarily interested in saleability, not the production of quality books. You could have written the best business book in a generation but if you are not well known or don't have a profile they feel they can exploit then you will find the process of securing a publisher far harder than the 19-year-old ex–Big Brother contestant who went through a sex change and wants to write their life story!

There is little doubt that some publishers still carry clout. For example, if your book is published by Harvard Business Review Press then you will gain a huge amount of credibility from that publisher. However, the chances of you securing a publishing contract with that publishing house are miniscule.

If you are seeking to work with blue-chip tier one organisations, then where your book is published may have an impact. However, I've never seen this play out in reality.

I wrote a book for a client in Australia and it was accepted by a top tier publisher with global reach. Naturally my client was over the moon. Unfortunately that publisher went through a strategic redirection handed down from global HQ which meant the contract was rescinded. Obviously my client was very disappointed and rather than go through the lengthy and tedious process of finding a new publisher, he decided to self-publish the book.

Limited by the technology at the time, there was no way this book could be mistaken for anything other than a self-published book. It didn't have an ISBN or barcode and there wasn't even any copy on the back cover or spine. And yet none of that made any difference to the increased credibility my client experienced as a result of the book. Prospects didn't care whether it was published by a traditional publisher or not, they read the material and resonated with the message. Has he sold millions of copies? Nowhere near, he'll have been lucky to have sold 1000 copies but it literally made him millions of dollars in new business! Interestingly we have since worked together again to create a second book which *is* published and there has been no discernible difference between the impact of the first book and the impact of the second book. Both books have fulfilled their purpose of increasing his credibility, reach and income.

There is, however, a very important caveat to add to this story – under no circumstances will you get away with such blatant self-publishing today.

And there is absolutely no excuse for it either. If you insist on cutting corners and focus on the product and not the quality of the writing and finished product then your book will look like a high school project and no amount of technology is going to save you.

If, however, you pay for the right expertise and ensure your book is properly edited, error-free and professionally designed and typeset then your self-published book can look indistinguishable from a traditionally published book. Done properly, self-published books no longer look self-published.

I have several clients who have decided to self-publish and looking at the book you wouldn't know the difference between that and a mainstream book. I also personally know one entrepreneur who featured as a contributor in a book on thought leadership which was published by a very small, unknown publishing house and it didn't stop her getting blue-chip clients. She is adamant that having the book opened doors which were previously bolted shut and it is that one strategy that revolutionised her business. We have since written her own book which was accepted by a traditional publisher based on her profile, her innovative methodology and the profile of the blue-chip companies she how serves.

The other issue that is often conveniently forgotten about when it comes to finding the right publisher is that very few people make their buying decision based on who published the book! I can't imagine for a minute, especially in business non-fiction, that a reader finds a book and decides not to buy it purely because it's NOT published by Harper Collins or John Wiley & Sons.

There was definitely a time where the credibility argument was valid and self-published books looked extremely amateur and unprofessional. But it's no longer accurate. Technology has improved out of sight both in terms of production and distribution and most people would not be able to differentiate between a book published by a traditional publisher and one which is self-published.

Authors are coming to realise they do have other viable options which would deliver all the advantages of a publishing contract with more of the revenue. Consequently, more and more authors are finally taking far greater control over their own publishing destiny.

Production

Production expertise and attention to detail is often another advantage given by the publishing houses to justify such small author royalties. And certainly once you've poured your heart and soul into your book and sent it off to them, they do take care of all the additional steps to get your book into the shops.

The publisher will appoint a production editor or desk editors who will co-ordinate the production of your book from copy-editing to proofreading to design and typesetting. They will also take care of cover design and take care of all the technical details such as getting an ISBN number and barcode for your book. This International Standard Book Number is a 10 or 13 digit number that identifies the book and is essential for distributors, booksellers and libraries. ISBN is an essential part of being taken seriously in the book world.

Production is a genuine advantage because there are many steps and people involved in creating the finished product. For example, books that are published by mainstream publishers will always adhere to the in-house style guide. The production editor will employ a copy-editor who will go through the manuscript to make sure that it adheres to this style guide. A copy-editor is focused on the "Five Cs" – to make the copy clear, correct, concise, complete and consistent.

The copy-editor doesn't change the content in the same way that a general editor would – they are focused on the detail so they are looking to correct spelling, punctuation, grammar, terminology, clarify or remove jargon, semantics and consistency. They will create more headings or standardise heading treatment and they will ensure that the text flows well and naturally and that what is being said is easy to follow and understand. The copy editor will bring a fresh eye to the book and make sure that your book is sensible, fair and accurate and they will flag any potential legal problems.

This copy-editing process is absolutely critical for the production of a great book. Too often authors choose to self-publish or go it alone and don't know about the role of the copy editor or they assume that their general editor will do all these things. They won't, unless you ask for copy-editing. I had one client who employed a well-known US editor to edit a book I'd written. As the book was targeted to the US market this was a smart move and I was reassured that he would do a great job. I didn't see the book again until it was printed. When I received the book it looked really fantastic. Then I started to read it. By the time I'd been through the whole book I'd found 1028 errors. I spoke to my client and he was pretty crestfallen. He had hired an experienced editor, but he didn't know about copy-editing and the need for a style guide. I had not flagged it because the US editor had considerable experience editing books so I just assumed he would take care of this but he did a general edit not a copy-edit. He was tightening up the copy and changing certain sections but he wasn't looking at the detail and the consistency of layout. In truth the vast majority of the 1028 errors were consistency issues or headings that were not the correct level. In other words most people who read the book would not notice the errors, but a professional would. Anyone inside the publishing industry, including professional book critics would have immediately known the book was self-published because of these errors – even though it looked like a high-end published book.

The production expertise that comes with a traditional publishing contract is invaluable so if you don't have the time or inclination to learn how to do it all yourself it's certainly a viable option – assuming you can get a publisher interested.

Having someone else deal with all the nitty-gritty details of publishing a book can be especially useful if you are running a busy business. If you consider that your main revenue will arrive in non-royalty based income, having a publisher handle everything so you can focus on cherry-picking the strategic advantages your book can give you, means you get most of the upside without the hassle. You may not make millions in royalties but if you can buy the books at wholesale and use them for business development purposes, you'll reap most of the rewards anyway.

Marketing

Marketing is another much discussed benefit of the traditional publishing model. When you are the author and your book is due for release the publisher will include that book in their catalogue and they will sell it into bookshops for you. They may also do their best to get you on TV shows and into magazines but the results are by no means guaranteed. Securing a publishing contract does not automatically mean that your book is going to sell like hot cakes. And don't for one second assume that a publisher's involvement means that you don't need to worry about marketing and selling your own book. The only person that can sell your book and make it a success is you. Having a publisher makes very little difference to this process.

From your side, your book is your primary focus – it's your baby and has perhaps taken years to birth. You are excited and enthusiastic and have high hopes for bestseller superstardom. From the publisher's side you are just one of many authors and many books launching at the same time. They will assign a certain time frame and budget to promotion and if the book gathers momentum they may get behind it with an extra push but if it doesn't take off they will move on to their next project without a backwards glance. It's a numbers game for the publishers.

No one knows what makes a bestseller a bestseller. There is no formula and no amount of publishing experience can predict it. It's random and comes down to luck, right timing, right topic and right market. The publisher knows that of all the books they choose only a small fraction will make money. It's a bit like a venture capitalist – they might invest in 30 businesses but they know that only two or three might make money but the money they will make in those two or three is so big it will offset the failure of the other 27 or 28 businesses. It's the same in publishing. Your publisher is hoping you sell millions of copies too and they will do their best to raise awareness of the book and generate sales, but if it doesn't they will be onto the next book hoping that one is "the one". The publisher only needs a few books to do really well and the rest can, and do, sink without a trace.

Disadvantages of Traditional Publishing

There are several disadvantages of traditional publishing but how much of a disadvantage these issues are will depend on the book, the author and what the author hopes to achieve from the book, and how he or she will use the content. For most authors the main disadvantages of traditional publishing are:

- Hard to Secure

- Long Lead Time

- Loss of Control

- Poor Financial Reward

Hard to Secure

The biggest downside regarding mainstream publishing is there are no guarantees your book will be selected for publication. Just because you think it's fabulous and harbour aspirations of securing a publishing contract, doesn't mean you will.

In truth, rejection is much more common than acceptance, especially with the top publishers. Most publishers don't accept unsolicited manuscripts. This means that if you send your *magnum opus* to would-be publishers "on spec" they won't even read it! To stand any chance of acceptance you need patience, you need to send a proposal which complies with their submission guidelines and you probably need to agree to buy some of your own books from the publisher.

The simple reality of publishing is that making money in books is not easy. Remember the sales figures from the UK which stated that of 86,000 new titles published in 2007 just over 58,000 of those sold an average of 18 copies. Publishers know that the top 5 percent of titles by sales volume will account for over 60 percent of total book sales.

US WRITERS MUST LEARN TO DEAL WITH REJECTION. PERSONALLY I FIND 3 DAYS ON THE COUCH, DAY-TIME TV AND AN EXTRA LARGE TUB OF MINT CHOC CHIP ICE CREAM DOES THE TRICK.

Long Lead Time

Just imagine – you've taken the time out and dedicated yourself to writing your book. It's been hard at times but as you look at your manuscript you're proud and excited about what you've created. If you haven't already started looking for a publishing house, you are about to find out that it can be a long and frustratingly silent process.

If you choose a large publisher, chances are they won't accept manuscripts unless submitted by an agent. Finding a good agent can be as hard, if not harder, than finding a publisher. If, by some miracle, your desired publisher does accept manuscripts without an agent then you could still be waiting up to six months for a response. And there are no guarantees that the eventual answer will be the one you want to hear.

Even if you have had the foresight to send out a proposal as you've been writing the book and even if, by some stroke of luck, genius or celebrity, you have secured a publisher prior to completing the manuscript, it will take up to 18 months from delivery of that manuscript to you seeing your book on the shelves of your local bookstore. It's not fast.

In the meantime there is nothing you can do. It's unlikely they will allow you to use excerpts from the book and you certainly won't be able to release an e-book version in the interim. So for one to two years you will not reap a single reward from all that work. Granted you could start calling yourself a "soon to be published author" but that will wear a bit thin after six months. This issue is being addressed by many of the big publishers in answer to the growth in self-publishing and print-on-demand (more on them in a moment) but traditional publishing is still not a particularly quick process. Even the quickest of the big publishers will take a minimum of six months.

Loss of Control

You may think that because you wrote your book that you own it and can do whatever you want with it. That would be logical but it's not accurate.

All books that are published have an ISBN number assigned to them. A paperback version of a book will have a different ISBN number to the hardback version so that the book industry can identify between books. When a traditional publisher publishes your book it will assign an ISBN number to your book. Whoever owns the ISBN owns the book. So if your book proved to be a sensation and Steven Spielberg wanted to negotiate film rights, legally he would have to negotiate with the publisher – not you. Unless you assign it elsewhere the author will always own the moral rights and copyright but that does not mean the author has control of that work. And few people realise this.

In addition, a standard publishing contract will usually be extremely limiting in where you can reproduce your own material. As a result you may very well lose a great deal of control and if you do end up going down this route make sure you have the contract looked over by a lawyer familiar with your plans and aspirations. If you know what you want to do with the book, for example if you want to use excerpts on your website or create special reports using some of the chapters, then you need to tell your lawyer as much detail as possible so he or she can trawl through the legal jargon and find out if it's allowed or not. It's safe to assume none of it will be allowed but if you know the deal up front then at least you can negotiate to have those sections removed instead of blindly signing the agreement and being upset later.

Pay particular attention to who owns the electronic rights and find out whether you can use excerpts of your own book or not. Are you, for example, allowed to re-create the material in other forms such as audio programs, podcasts etc.? What about overseas rights? All contracts are written in favour of the person who creates the contract – publishing is no exception. The clearer you are about what it is you are trying to achieve with the book and all the possible uses you may have for it the more likely you are to avoid problems in the future. If you envisage wanting to create special reports that use extracts from the book, then make sure that is allowed in the contract. If you envisage YouTube style video messages or podcasts or you want to incorporate some of the content in your web blog then negotiate these things at the start.

If you don't think about these issues and negotiate specific allowances for them in the contract then it's virtually guaranteed you'll run into problems later. That is why knowing your strategy is so important. Try to envisage how you may want to use your own product in the future so that you don't get roasted by the publisher.

In addition, you may have very clear ideas about the title and cover design but you might find yourself in a losing battle. To be fair, in this instance the publisher will have expertise that you should probably trust.

You need to understand that without any challenge to the publisher's contract, you will be giving away a great deal of control over your book – how it looks and how you can use it for your own benefit in your business. So be careful what you sign.

Poor Financial Rewards

In the traditional publishing model, if you write a book and were lucky enough to get your book accepted by a mainstream publisher through a well-connected agent, contact or other miracle, you might receive 10 to 15 percent royalty as a new author. You may be a little disappointed and think it pretty lame when you consider how much effort and intellectual property has gone into it.

But it's actually worse than you think! That new author (or indeed any author) will receive 10 to 15 percent of *net receipts,* not the recommended retail price or sale price. Basically a publisher will sell your book to bookshops for up to 60 percent less than the recommended book price. So your royalty isn't payable on sale price but wholesale price. Using the exchange rate at the time of writing and assuming you have managed to secure the best possible royalty of 15 percent royalty, the table below will give you an idea of what you can expect...

	Jacket Price	Bookshop Discount (Up to 60 percent)	Net Receipts	Author Royalty per book (15 percent)	Author income at 5,000 copies	Author income at 10,000 copies
UK	£14.95	£8.97	£5.98	£0.897	£4,485	£8,970
US	$23.47	$14.08	$9.39	$1.408	$7,040	$14,080
Australia	$23.79	$14.27	$9.52	$1.428	$7,140	$14,280

In Australia if a book sold 5,000 copies it would be considered a bestseller. Granted, Australia is a small market but if you sold 10,000 copies through a bookstore in the UK or 30,000 in the US, most publishers would consider that a success. In any country, on any topic, if a non-fiction book sold 7,500 copies it would be considered successful. It may not be a bestseller on those sales but it would be considered a success. You need to know this so that you don't get upset later on. When people write for the money they are invariably disappointed. Dreams of topping the *New York Times* Best Sellers list, early retirement and a life of luxury in Barbados give way to a caravan by the coast for two weeks a year!

When you consider that millions of books are being published every year, there really are very, *very* few authors who ever make serious money from royalty income alone.

Plus even if your book does sell well don't expect to receive your royalty cheque quickly. All high street booksellers work on a sale or return basis, which means that they will only stock your book in their shop if they have the option to return it to the publisher should it not sell. Obviously publishers don't want to pay royalty income on books that have not sold. They will therefore wait to make sure that the books distributed have actually sold and are not returned to their warehouse which means you have to wait too.

You've probably guessed by now that I'm not a huge fan of traditional publishing. But to be fair it is the booksellers that take the least risk and potentially make the most money. If you consider that books are sold into bookshops for up to 60 percent discount on the anticipated recommended retail price it is the booksellers that stand to make the most money. The bookshops don't always sell those books at jacket price and will often have to discount books to make the sale but with a sale or return policy they also have the least risk.

The crux of the matter is that if you choose to take the traditional publishing route then there are many stakeholders in the process that must be paid before you. Both publishers and the booksellers have significant overheads including staff, office or retail costs. Consequently, if you take this option these stakeholders are ahead of you in the payment queue and will take their cut long before you receive anything.

Who Is Best Suited to Traditional Publishing?

Whether or not traditional publishing is for you or not depends on your book, your profile, your current workload and what you want to do with the book. There are times when securing a traditional publisher *is* the best option, assuming you can get a publisher interested. Traditional publishing may be right for you if:

- You don't have the time or inclination to get involved in the processes beyond the actual writing.

- You don't mind the long lead time or would prefer a long lead time.

- You have your heart set on a mainstream publisher and nothing else will do.

- You have a great agent or connections in the publishing industry that can get your manuscript read.

- Royalty income is not the motivation for writing the book.

Who Are Traditional Publishers Most Interested In?

The publishing industry is changing but securing a traditional publishing contract is as difficult as ever. Like all businesses they are looking for products that will sell and ways to reduce their risk. They will therefore be more interested in you and your book if:

- You are prepared to sell your own book over and above any publisher involvement.

- You are a "big fish" either in a little or large pond!

- You have a celebrity status or a large "natural market".

- You have an engaging "hook" or new way of presenting topical information.

- You have access to celebrity endorsement.

- You are prepared to buy back a significant number of your own books.

If you are planning to write a few books and you already have a natural market or an existing "platform" then you need to think long and hard about traditional publishing. If you have a large client database or frequently speak at seminars or events then you could make a great deal more money going it alone. However, if money is not your motivation and you just want the book without getting involved in the minutia of publishing then use that natural market to bargain with the publisher to increase your royalty AND negotiate a discount on the books so that you can buy in bulk and onsell at events. That way, you still get the mainstream publisher but can also gain some of the financial upside which is only fair if you are selling the majority of the books yourself!

Securing a Traditional Publishing Contract

If you are committed to this route then buy a copy of either the *Writers' and Artists' Yearbook* or *The Writers Market*. Both books are fully revised and updated every year and contain detailed information about publishers and agents. Publisher information includes address and contact details, contact person, how many titles they publish each year, what genre they publish, together with submission guidelines. These books also include valuable essays from successful writers and cover information such as copyright, libel and tax issues. In short, one or the other of these comprehensive guides is essential if you are serious about finding a mainstream publisher.

Publisher Hierarchy

There are literally thousands of publishers but not all publishers are equal. In broad terms they are split into a hierarchy of importance. At the top of the publishing tree are "tier one" publishers. These publishers and their various imprints are considered the best, largest and/or most prestigious publishers in the world.

Tier one publishers include:

- John Wiley & Sons

- Random House

- HarperCollins

- McGraw-Hill

- Pearson

- Simon & Schuster

- Scholastic

- Harvard Business Review Press

- Holtzbrinck Publishing Holdings

- Time Warner

Many of the large publishers have multiple imprints, for example Pearson own Financial Times Group, Pearson Education and Penguin – each a major publishing organisations in its own right.

Beyond that there are "tier two" and "tier three" publishers and the list of both is exhaustive so I won't include it here. Besides, there is some debate about which publishers fall into what category. To give you an idea, according to *Publishers Weekly* there are about 400 medium sized publishers and up to 86,000 small publishers in the US alone!

The best thing to do is to buy a copy of either of the reference guides mentioned earlier and work your way through the book to identify which publishers would be interested in publishing your type of book. Alternatively, find out who published the books you admire and research those publishers. Both techniques will immediately narrow the field. Then you can do some research on each company. Look at what titles they have published that are similar to your book, find out how many books they publish each year and draw up a short list of your "preferred publishers" including order of preference. If possible, find out when they make their publishing choices for the year so you can time your approach accordingly.

Of course, just because you decide that only a "tier one" publisher will do does not mean you will actually secure one. It's not easy. First you need to get the publisher's submission guidelines which are usually available on the publisher's website. Follow the submission guidelines exactly and use contacts you have to get your manuscript read. Publishers are inundated by unsolicited manuscripts; as a result most are never read. According to BookStatistics.com, Peachtree Publishers, one of the last publishers in the US to accept unsolicited manuscripts, receives up to 25,000 per year and yet they publish just 20. You will never secure a publishing deal with a top tier publisher by sending an unsolicited manuscript. Most large publishers won't even accept a proposal unless it's presented by an agent.

One possible way around this, but it's by no means guaranteed, is to find someone who has been published by the company you would like to be published with and seek an introduction. Publishing is like everything else in life – it's not what you know, it's who you know! Without an agent or a personal introduction you will be struggling even to get your manuscript read.

Preparing a Publishing Proposal

Most publishers will want a proposal. If you have decided that the only way you will write the book is if you can get a publishing deal then you need to start this process sooner rather than later. Make sure you get the specific submission details from your chosen publisher but, as a guide, they will want:

- An executive summary.

- Who are you and what qualifies you to write this book?

- Do you have a natural market? If so, can you estimate how many books you could sell to that market? Be realistic – even 1000 would make a big difference to a publisher.

- Target audience and competitor books. What other successful books have been written already that are similar to your idea and what makes your book different and better. This sounds contradictory but publishers are most interested in backing books that are low risk. That means they want assurances that the topic is selling in a successful genre. They also want to know what makes your book different so that they can be assured it will stand out in that market and sell well.

- The author promotional plan. What are you prepared to do to market your book? Will you be available for interviews, TV and radio? Will you be presenting at events, conferences and seminars?

- Do you have any celebrity status that could help sell the book? Or do you know someone that could endorse your book on the cover? The word "celebrity" in this context means someone with either real or perceived weight with the audience – so a sports star, academic, other well-known author, scientist or appropriate celebrity that the readers would recognise.

- Specifications – what will the format be? Initial hardcover followed by soft cover or straight to soft cover? What size will it be, how long and when will the manuscript be finished?

- Are you writing the book yourself? If so, have you written anything else and has it been published? If you are not writing the book yourself are you using a recognised ghostwriter? This can be appealing to the publisher because they can count on a certain standard of writing quality and that deadlines will be met. Writers are notorious for missing deadlines and it doesn't make them popular with their publisher. It has serious repercussions for the publisher so any assurances that this won't happen will be welcome news.

I have a proven track record with several publishers and consequently I am able to get manuscripts I write for clients read by the relevant commissioning editor. There are no guarantees with this approach but considering the size of the slush pile and the need for agent submissions, this can be a massive advantage that a ghostwriter may bring to the table beyond the actual writing.

The proposal must also include:

- Table of Contents

- Chapter summaries describing the take-away value of each chapter

- Introduction

- Sample chapters

A good publisher can be a real asset especially if you are already busy running a business and you don't have the time or inclination to learn how to publish your book yourself. But you need to enter the agreement with your eyes wide open.

Personally, I think the mainstream publishing route holds little genuine advantage for the vast majority of authors. There are too many people in the pipeline to be paid before the author receives any real benefit. A huge part of this is simple supply and demand – every man and his dog wants to write a book! The state of the publishing world is therefore a consequence of evolution, not some vindictive plan to exploit authors! For decades publishing companies have been able to pick and choose their business. Sometimes they get it right and sometimes they don't. Publishers are by no means infallible. There is no known formula for a bestseller. The book buying public is fickle and even the big guns get it wrong occasionally. Many classic books have been repeatedly rejected before finding fame and fortune. Margaret Mitchell's *Gone with the Wind* was rejected 38 times, Stephen King's *Carrie* was turned down 30 times and E. E. Cummings' *The Enormous Room*, now considered a masterpiece, was ultimately self-published and dedicated to the 15 publishers who rejected it. Even the legendary J. K. Rowling's *Harry Potter* was turned down 12 times before Bloomsbury picked it up! Spotting a winner is not always easy.

However, this oversupply of "talent" gives the publishers all the power and it has created a highly skewed system. From a publisher's perspective, the author can't do it without them. From an author's perspective, a publisher would have nothing to take to market without them. So there are definitely two sides to this old story. As author Doris Lessing says, *"It does no harm to repeat, as often as you can, 'Without me the literary industry would not exist: the publishers, the agents, the sub-agents, the accountants, the libel lawyers, the departments of literature, the professors, the theses, the books of criticism, the reviewers, the book pages – all this vast and proliferating edifice is because of this small, patronised, put-down and underpaid person.'"*

The balance of power is, however, shifting due to the phenomenal advances in technology and the opportunities presented by the Internet. There is, for example, now a book printing machine which has been hailed as the ATM for books. The Espresso Book Machine looks like a large photocopier and was named as one of the best inventions of 2008 by *Time* magazine. The aptly named Espresso can print a 300-page paperback, complete with colour cover, in just 3 minutes. Simply upload the files and your book will be printed by the time you've finished your latte.

The Internet is also taking the edge off traditional publishing's unique selling proposition (USP). Twenty years ago, if you wanted your book in front of potential buyers you had to secure a traditional publishing contract. Now the Internet reaches billions of people around the world and the old rules no longer apply. This has opened up new markets and delivery channels which are offering authors exciting new opportunities for sales and distribution. For example, electronic delivery is changing the way we buy information and that is particularly relevant in the business sector.

Today there are many more ways to effectively skin the publishing and bookselling cat! As a result, many of the traditional publishers – especially the smaller ones – are opening their doors to partnership arrangements. This means that you can have your book published the traditional way in exchange for agreeing to buy a certain quantity of books from the initial print-run. This is not vanity publishing because the publisher will treat your book as though it was one of their selected titles and will do all they can to sell and distribute the title – something that vanity publishers will not do.

This can be a great solution for people who just want an established imprint and don't have the time or inclination to see to all the details. These publishers obviously have a great deal of experience and can really make your book look fantastic, but it's not necessarily a cheap option. The publishing industry is changing rapidly so I've not included which publishers are offering this solution as they may not be offering it tomorrow. Instead email me at karen@wordarchitect.com and I'll tell you the ones I know about at the time. Alternatively simply choose the publisher you would like to partner with and approach them directly with the request. You never know unless you ask!

Summary of Key Points

- In the past the only way you could be published was by convincing a publisher of the merits of your book.

- To automatically assume that some big publisher will snap up your manuscript with verve and passion and you'll make millions in royalty income is pure fiction.

- There are several advantages of having your book published by a large well-known traditional publisher, but the most significant are credibility, production and marketing.

- Credibility is the main advantage touted by traditional publishing. According to the publishing industry a book published with them has more credibility and kudos than a book which is self-published.

- The reality, however, is a little different. For a start, mainstream publishers don't really assess on quality they assess on saleability.

- You could have written the best business book in a generation but if you are not well known or don't have a profile they feel they can exploit then you will find the process of securing a publisher far harder than the 19-year-old ex–Big Brother contestant who went through a sex change and wants to write their life story!

- There is little doubt that some publishers still carry clout. If you are seeking to work with blue-chip tier one organisations then where your book is published may have an impact.

- There was definitely a time where the credibility argument was valid and self-published books looked extremely amateur and unprofessional. But it's no longer accurate.

- Production expertise and attention to detail is often another advantage given by the publishing houses to justify such small author royalties.

- The publisher will appoint a production editor or desk editors who will co-ordinate the production of your book from copy-editing to proofreading to design and typesetting.

- The production expertise that comes with a traditional publishing contract is invaluable so if you don't have the time or inclination to learn how to do it all yourself it's certainly a viable option – assuming you can get a publisher interested.

- Marketing is another much discussed benefit of the traditional publishing model. When you are the author and your book is due for release the publisher will include that book in their catalogue and they will sell it into bookshops for you.

- They may also do their best to get you on TV shows and into magazines but the results are by no means guaranteed. Securing a publishing contract does not automatically mean that your book is going to sell like hotcakes.

- For most authors the main disadvantages of traditional publishing are: hard to secure, long lead time, loss of control and poor financial rewards.

- The biggest downside regarding mainstream publishing is there are no guarantees your book will be selected for publication. Just because you think it's fabulous and harbour aspirations of securing a publishing contract doesn't mean you will.

- It will take up to 18 months from delivery of that manuscript to you seeing your book on the shelves of your local bookstore.

- Even the quickest of the big publishers will take a minimum of six months.

- You may think that because you wrote your book that you own it and can do whatever you want with it. That would be logical but it's not accurate.

- Whoever owns the ISBN owns the book. So if your book proved to be a sensation and Steven Spielberg wanted to negotiate film rights legally he would have to negotiate with the publisher – not you.

- Unless you assign it elsewhere the author will always own the moral rights and copyright but that does not mean the author has control of that work.

- If you write a book and were lucky enough to get your book accepted by a mainstream publisher you might receive a 10 to 15 percent royalty as a new author.

- That new author (or indeed any author) will receive 10 to 15 percent of *net receipts*, not the recommended retail price or sale price.

- When you consider that millions of books are being published every year, there really are very, *very* few authors who ever make serious money from royalty income alone.

- Traditional publishing may be right for you if you don't have the time or inclination to get involved in the processes beyond the actual writing. You don't mind the long lead time or you have your heart set on a mainstream publisher and nothing else will do. You have connections and royalty income is not the motivation for writing the book.

- A large publisher will be more interested in you and your book if you are prepared to sell your own book, you are a "big fish", have celebrity status or a large "natural market", if you have an engaging "hook" or new way of presenting topical information, access of celebrity endorsement and are prepared to buy back a significant number of your own books.

- If you are committed to this route then buy a copy of either the *Writers' and Artists' Yearbook* or *The Writers Market*. Both books are fully revised and updated every year and contain detailed information about publishers and agents.

- Work your way through the book to identify which publishers would be interested in publishing your type of book. Alternatively, find out who published the books you admire and research those publishers. Both techniques will immediately narrow the field.

- You will never secure a publishing deal with a top tier publisher by sending an unsolicited manuscript. Most large publishers won't even accept a proposal unless it's presented by an agent.

- A good publisher can be a real asset especially if you are already busy running a business and you don't have the time or inclination to learn how to publish your book yourself. But you need to enter the agreement with your eyes wide open.

- Today there are many more ways to effectively skin the publishing and bookselling cat! As a result, many of the traditional publishers – especially the smaller ones – are opening their doors to partnership arrangements.

Chapter 15
The Other Way – Self-Publishing

*The self-publisher really has control of his or her
destiny to a much larger degree than does a writer
merely submitting a manuscript [to a publisher].*
~ Dan Poynter

Things are changing and the traditional publishing model is no longer the only way to get your book in front of your audience. In the old model, if a publisher didn't accept your book there was no other course of action open to you. Yet traditional publishers have repeatedly rejected many of the most successful books of all time. Those authors have had enough faith in their own work to seek alternative ways and sometimes that faith has paid off. A desire to take control of their publishing destiny (regardless of what the mainstream publishers said), improvements in technology and innovations in distribution channels have led to the development of other alternatives, such as self-publishing.

Self-publishing is not new, it's been around a long time, but it's only just started to look good! Initially it was lame. The books often looked more like a school project and the binding and artwork was poor. But all that is in the distant past. Unfortunately some of the stigma attached to self-publishing remains today, especially if you are talking to mainstream publishers!

Self-publishing is exactly what it says on the tin – where you take over all the tasks that were traditionally done by the publishing house. That means being in charge of editing, copy-editing, proofreading, design, layout, indexing, securing an ISBN and barcode. Then on top of all that you need to find a printer to create the finished product. And that's just to get the book – you then have to distribute it and sell it.

Needless to say, self-publishing is not for the busy or faint-hearted!

Advantages of Self-Publishing

Self-publishing has a number of advantages but the most significant ones are:

- Total Control

- Greater Revenue

- Future Potential

Total Control

The obvious advantage of self-publishing is that you retain full control of your own book. If you are undaunted by the task ahead, self-publishing can offer a unique opportunity for you to create exactly the book you want without outside interference.

Having total control however means that you really do need to know the process. The reality is that self-published books that *look* self-published look self-published because the person managing the process doesn't understand the necessary steps between the finished manuscript and point of sale. You absolutely need to appreciate the stages and steps that you need to go through otherwise you could make some major mistakes. Self-publishing, therefore, is only really an option if you are prepared to immerse yourself in the process and understand what needs to happen *before* you start.

Once you have finished writing the book you will need to have it professionally edited. That person will tighten up the writing and just make the book better. And they will correct any glaring errors of syntax, sense, spelling and grammar. This initial edit is to assess that the book works and makes sense, that the order and structure works and that the book flows well and logically.

After the general edit you will need to employ a copy-editor who will review the book line by line to make sure everything is clear, correct, concise, complete, and consistent. This editor will need to know your "house style" or what style guide you are using. Every traditional publishing house has a house style or follows a particular style guide. For example, if you picked up any book published by John Wiley & Sons or a particular imprint within a large publishing house all the books regardless of the author follow a house style. This means that every book that is published by that publisher or under that imprint will look like it belongs to the same family. That cohesion is not an accident. Each book will follow the same rules in terms of how the book looks in print. The house style will cover everything from spelling conventions to when to use italics to heading conventions to font and point size. If you look at grammar rules, for example, there are often several right ways to deal with certain situations but using more than one right way in one book makes both ways wrong. The key is choosing a rule and applying that rule consistently. The copy-editor will need to know what your house style is so that he or she can ensure that your manuscript meets those rules.

If you are only going to publish one book then you don't necessarily need a house style but if you intend to publish more than one book then you do. You want all the books you create to look as though they belong to the same family. If you don't have a house style then find someone who has experience copy-editing books for mainstream publishers and simply ask them to edit to a style they are familiar with.

Assuming you and the various editors have also been watching out for typos and spelling mistakes you then need to pass your manuscript to a designer who will design a cover and create a matching page layout and text design that ensures the book looks like a coherent product. You will also need to supply back cover copy for your book. This needs to be punchy and appealing so that you attract the attention of would-be readers. Once the design has been agreed and finalised the manuscript is then sent on to the typesetter who sets the type on the page for production. The typesetter will create a page proof of each page – this is exactly how the book will look when it's printed. These page proofs will be sent back to you to check. By this time you will be sick of the sight of your book and the last thing you will want to do is read it again. But you have to.

While you are reading it again you also need to pass it to a professional proofreader who has never seen the book before. Sometimes in the typesetting stage as the text is being moved about and manipulated small errors can creep into the book so it is absolutely vital that you get a fresh pair of eyes on the manuscript prior to print. Ultimately it is your responsibility to make sure the book is error-free and you need to employ professionals to help you ensure that outcome.

Also you need to check all the cross referencing points in your book. For example you may have written, "remember on page 17, we talked about diversification...". When you were writing the book it may have been page 17 on your word processing document but now that the book is designed and typeset around a particular book size it may be page 34. You need to check all the cross references in the book to ensure their accuracy.

While you and the proofreader are making the final pass you need to send the proofs to a professional indexer who will create an index for the book. Ideally the indexer should be a specialist in your area so they can create the most useful index but it's not absolutely necessary. This will cost very little and adds a huge amount of credibility and professionalism to a non-fiction book.

Remember this is not an opportunity to make changes; any change you make may push out the layout and render the index invalid so where possible leave the book alone and simply make sure what is written is accurate. If you do end up making changes, perhaps new research has emerged as your book has been edited, then expect to pay for those changes over and above any agreed price.

You also need to apply for an ISBN and create a barcode for your book. This is done via Nielsen and you will need to register as a publisher. The minimum number of ISBNs you can apply for is 10 but that may change.

Once everything has been finished and you are happy with the manuscript and how the book will look *you* will be asked to sign off the proofs ready for production. This means that if there is a mistake that you have missed on the proofs it's your fault and not the printers.

This can be a nerve-racking moment but if you have employed professionals and read and reread your book yourself then you have done everything you can. Take a deep breath and sign if off ready for print.

Then you just wait for the finished product to arrive and bask in the warm glow of authorship!

As you can see, total control is a lot of work, attention to detail and co-ordination. If you chose to self-publish in any way – whether printing 2,000 books up-front or using print-on-demand or e-publishing technology you need to follow this process to ensure an error-free professional outcome.

Greater Revenue

As I mentioned earlier, if you use a traditional publisher you immediately put more stakeholders into the payment chain and they are all paid before you are. Self-publishing removes those "middle men" and allows you to negotiate directly with those actually making the book. By speaking directly to editors, proofreaders, designers and printers you can manage the unit cost yourself. Providing you can effectively sell the books you are therefore in a better position to keep more of the revenue. With more control over costs and sales you can maintain a healthy margin and reap more of the financial reward.

However selling books is not easy. Most people grossly overestimate how many books they will actually sell.

Future Potential

Once you have scaled the steep learning curve, self-publishing does offer a significant revenue stream if you feel you have half a dozen books in you and have a large natural market.

It could also offer a future business development opportunity if you later meet others who could benefit from your publishing expertise.

Disadvantages of Self-Publishing

Before you decide that self-publishing is the perfect solution you need to be aware of the disadvantages. The main disadvantages are:

- Total Control

- Significant Up-Front Costs

- Sales

Total Control

This is either the biggest advantage or the biggest disadvantage depending on your perspective. Publishing is not a simple three-step process – each stage of writing, publishing and selling has a great deal to it. Just how much was explained under this same heading for the advantages of self-publishing. You have to organise and pay for an editor, copy-editor, proofreader, indexer, designer for the cover, typesetter to lay out the book ready for printing, you need to apply for an ISBN and get a barcode, you need to keep on the right side of legislation and then you have to be a printing expert and negotiate best rates.

And to top it all off you then need to understand the various distribution channels so that your book can be found by would-be readers and easily purchased.

Significant Up-Front Costs

Because you are responsible for everything, you have to pay for everything. There are book preparation costs that can't be avoided. Trying to cut corners is a fatal mistake. If you are the writer of your book then you CAN'T effectively edit the book. You need a professional copy-editor and a proofreader to check the manuscript. There is nothing that screams amateur louder than a spelling mistake! All your effort will be in vain the moment your reader finds an error and that's an incredibly high price to pay just to save a few shekels!

There are also book creation costs. The best-case scenario is that you will need to print at least 2,000 books in order to achieve a realistic unit cost. Getting everything right does cost money. And then you've still got to sell them!

Sales

In the traditional publishing model, distribution and therefore sales is all part of the contract. The publisher will therefore get your book into all the selling channels as part of their involvement.

Self-publishing on the other hand means you're on your own and that can be very dangerous. Unless you know what you're doing or have a large database or speak at regular events, you risk ending up with a garage full of books!

Ideally you want to make your book available to the widest possible audience. The virtue of having your own book as a business development tool doesn't depend on large sales but it always adds credibility if you can direct a would-be client to Amazon or their local bookshop to buy your book.

Who Is Best Suited to Self-Publishing?

Like traditional publishing, whether self-publishing is for you or not depends on your book, your profile, your current workload and what you want to do with the book. Self-publishing may be right for you if:

- You have plenty of cash.

- You have plenty of time.

- You see a long-term value and use in the knowledge and expertise you could gain from self-publishing.

- You have plans for several books and a guaranteed way of selling at least enough to make it viable.

- Your business is content-rich and in-house publication could be a lucrative sideline.

Basically self-publishing is the control freak's answer to publishing. It's a serious amount of work for one person to undertake and if you are already running a successful business it's not really viable. Especially when you consider that your intention is probably not to sell millions of copies (although that would be nice) but rather to create business development opportunities. Self-publishing, in this context, is therefore probably not the best option. The only exception to that is if you plan to launch a speaking career, or if you are already an established speaker in need of books and product to sell to a thriving and motivated audience. Otherwise, there is a far better option which I will discuss in the next chapter.

Summary of Key Points

- Self-publishing is not new, it's been around a long time but it's only just started to look good! Initially it was lame. The books often looked more like a school project and the binding and artwork was poor.

- Self-publishing is exactly what it says on the tin – where you take over all the tasks that were traditionally done by the publishing house. That means being in charge of editing, copy-editing, proofreading, design, layout, indexing, and securing an ISBN and barcode.

- Self-publishing has a number of advantages but the most significant ones are total control, greater revenue and future potential.

- The obvious advantage of self-publishing is that you retain full control of your own book.

- With more control over costs and sales you can maintain a healthy margin and reap more of the financial reward.

- Once you have scaled the steep learning curve, self-publishing does offer a significant revenue stream if you feel you have half a dozen books in you and have a large natural market.

- Before you decide that self-publishing is the perfect solution you need to be aware of the disadvantages which are total control, significant up-front costs, and sales.

- This is either the biggest advantage or the biggest disadvantage depending on your perspective. Publishing is not a simple three-step process – each stage of writing, publishing and selling has a great deal to it.

- And to top it all off you then need to understand the various distribution channels so that your book can be found by would-be readers and easily purchased.

- Because you are responsible for everything, you have to pay for everything. There are book preparation costs that can't be avoided. Trying to cut corners is a fatal mistake.

- When it comes to distribution and sales with self-publishing you're on your own and that can be very dangerous. Unless you know what you're doing or have a large database or speak at regular events, you risk ending up with a garage full of books!

- Self-publishing may be right for you if you have plenty of cash and time. You see a long-term value and use in the knowledge and expertise you could gain from self-publishing and you plan to write several books or your business is content-rich and in-house publication could be a lucrative sideline.

- Basically self-publishing is the control freak's answer to publishing. It's a serious amount of work for one person to undertake and if you are already running a successful business it's not really viable.

Chapter 16

The New Way – Print-On-Demand (POD)

Innovation is the creation of the new or the
re-arranging of the old in a new way.
~ Michael Vance

Print-on-demand (POD) is the most exciting thing to happen to authors since the Biro or the memory stick! Even mainstream publishers are excited – although for different reasons. One of the most popular arguments used by publishers about why they can't pay their authors more in royalties is because of the cost and risk of printing the books up-front. In the traditional model, the publisher must gauge from experience and pre-sales figures how many books to produce in the initial print run. Too few and the unit price is needlessly high and too many and they risk having to pulp hundreds, possibly thousands, of books. In 2007, according to BookStatistics.com 40 percent of manufactured books in the US never sold and were subsequently destroyed. That's a lot of books!

However, publishers are now able to use POD technology so they don't have to carry the risk of large up-front print runs. This means that the only books that are printed are books that have already been sold! They will of course need to print extra to supply bookstores but the quantities and risk becomes significantly lower. From an environmental perspective this is great news, but to use it as justification for poor royalties is a little rich.

So what is print-on-demand? Exactly what it says it is. The book will only be printed when there is a demand for it.

Instead of handing your manuscript over to a publisher you simply upload your files to the POD company. They prepare your book for publication and get the book listed with all the big sellers including major online retailers like Amazon. Then you put the kettle on and wait for a sale.

When someone finds your book and orders it, the POD company processes the payment, prints the book and delivers it to the customer. You pay for the printing cost but only for the books that are sold and you receive a royalty on the sale. In addition, if you want a quantity of your own books for promotional purposes, or to sell to your existing contacts or at seminars and events, you simply pay the cost price of printing and delivery. That way you can enjoy an even higher margin on books you sell yourself.

There are a number of POD companies out there – the big ones are CreateSpace (formerly known as BookSurge) and Lightening Source Incorporated (LSI).

CreateSpace is Amazon's POD division which allows them to increase their influence right along the supply chain. Books created by CreateSpace are then sold through the Amazon network. If you want to use CreateSpace there is online support and tutorials available to help you through the preparation and submission process. You do have to get this right and closely manage the process otherwise you will be charged extra for amendments.

LSI is owned by Ingram Industries who have a vast distribution network both on and offline. Ingram is a respected name in publishing with a massive reach, ensuring that you get your book in front of 80 percent of all book wholesalers and retailers! That's even bigger than Amazon.

It is worth pointing out, however, that Lightening Source do not get involved with individual authors. LSI is the Grandfather of POD technology and has the most experience – but they only deal with publishers. You might think this is unfair but they are suppliers and don't want to diversify into author management. Which, let's face it, can be a challenging task. As writers, we get attached to our work and we want to ask questions – usually lots of questions! LSI doesn't want to have to educate authors in all sorts of technical production issues and have made the smart, strategic choice to stick to what they do best – production and distribution. Instead, they direct authors to a number of author services companies that will help you transform your manuscript into a finished product and project manage the whole process for you.

For this book I used a company called BookPOD based in Melbourne, Australia (www.bookpod.com.au). I have been recommending them to clients in the UK, Australia and USA for many years. They really know their way around POD and specifically how to upload the files correctly. I could have taken the time out to learn how to do it myself but I preferred to get an expert to do it for me. That way I can concentrate on the writing and let someone I trust take care of the rest.

Advantages of Print-On-Demand

There are significant advantages of print-on-demand that make it superior to self-publishing. The main advantages are:

- Lower Up-Front Costs

- Flexibility

- Access to Sales Channels

- POD Is Environmentally Friendly

- Fast and Credible

Low Up-Front Costs

Theoretically all you need to do is supply the POD company with your manuscript. Each company is slightly different but in essence you pay a fee for uploading the file. The size of that fee depends on how much you want the POD company to do and how much you have done yourself. For example, you can provide a word processed file and create your book from template designs or have something custom designed. Or you can go through the same process as self-publishing and more closely control the finished product and upload the files as a print-ready PDF or alternative print-ready file.

In other words you would run through the process described on page 198 - 201 so that you have a signed off proof. Instead of converting that proof to a file for physical printing by a book printer the file would be converted so it could be uploaded to the print-on-demand provider.

You may be tempted to go for the cheaper looking option which is to upload a Word file and complete the book from a template design. But be warned, most POD companies have a strict set of specifications and requirements and you will be charged extra if you don't meet them. Providing a print-ready file will always give you the greatest control over how the book will look and although there are costs incurred they are worth it to ensure an error-free finished product that you can be proud of.

Regardless of how you choose to upload the files or what services you choose from your POD company, it's much less expensive than self-publishing. There is no major investment required to print 2000 books up-front as you only pay for printing when the book is ordered.

Flexibility

What you write is not set in stone. The books are only printed when someone orders that book so there are not thousands of pre-printed books sitting in a warehouse. That means if something in your book suddenly changes, for example, advice you give is no longer accurate because of changing legislation, then you can just change the files. You don't have to keep a dated book, instead you make the changes to the POD file, call the book a revised or 2nd edition and the customer gets an updated, accurate book. All without having to pulp a single copy!

You can even get really clever and personalise bits of your book to particular market segments in your target market. For example, I saw a book on how to build a website using open source software and you could choose your industry from a long list of possibilities so that all the examples used to illustrate points were directly relevant to that industry. Now that's target marketing! Basically 90 percent of the book would be the same but the remaining 10 percent would be personalised to a particular audience.

Access to Sales Channels

A great POD company will get your book listed with all the major distributors and booksellers so the sales problem of self-publishing is at least partially overcome. Selling the book is probably the hardest part, so having this done for you is a *major* benefit.

You will always have to sell your own book but having it available through a wide variety of sales channels is imperative. It also lifts your credibility if you can say, "If you want more copies, you can get them from Amazon." Being able to direct people to recognised booksellers or online stores where they can either buy the electronic book or have it delivered in a few days is professional and adds to your status as an author.

POD Is Environmentally Friendly

POD is much more environmentally friendly than printing thousands of books that you *hope* you'll sell. The books are only printed when there is an order so there is no inventory, no waste and no garage full of unwanted books!

Fast and Credible

You could have a physical book in your hand within weeks of finishing the manuscript. Compare that to the traditional publishing model and it's a clear winner. Think of all the business you could be losing while you wait up to 18 months *after* you've finished the manuscript before you see your book in print.

And for those that are worried about the quality of POD books... I've bought several and have clients that have taken this route and seriously you wouldn't know the difference. The quality of print and finish is indistinguishable from traditional publishing.

Disadvantages of Print-On-Demand

There are very few *real* disadvantages of print-on-demand but the sceptics will tell you that the main disadvantages are:

- Lower Profit Margin

- Possible Contract Issues

- Reputation Question Marks

Lower Profit Margin

All of POD's considerable advantages do however come at a price and you will enjoy a lower profit margin than self-publishing. Print-on-demand companies effectively do everything a traditional publisher does except marketing and yet you will receive about 35 percent in royalty as opposed to 10 – 15 percent. That's two or three times what a traditional publisher will pay you!

You may potentially keep more of the revenue from self-publishing but you have to consider how many books you will sell on your own... 100 percent of nothing is still nothing. Better to go for a smaller slice of a bigger pie. Besides, like the publisher, the POD company is producing and delivering your book so there are costs associated with that effort.

Possible Contract Issues

Contracts are always written in favour of the person providing the contract and that is true of POD. Some contracts can therefore be restrictive, so make sure you read the contract thoroughly, ask for clarification on issues you're unclear of, and never be afraid to negotiate.

It's always wise to have a lawyer look at the contract, preferably one that understands your business and what you are trying to achieve with the book.

Reputation Question Marks

Questions have been raised about POD's reputation – but again I don't believe this is valid. POD has come on in leaps and bounds over the past few years and most people wouldn't even be able to tell the difference between a POD book and a book published by a major publisher.

Print-on-demand is certainly the most exciting thing to happen to publishing for a long time and it finally offers authors a legitimate avenue to get a professional-looking physical product without selling their soul to get it. There are those that say that POD books lack bookstore credibility but that's what they said about self-publishing and many world famous authors self-published and went on to great things. Wayne Dyer started his career by self-publishing his work and selling it out of a Combi van – he's now worth millions. James Redfield's *Celestine Prophecy* was initially turned down by several publishers so he self-published and sold it himself, and again he's worth millions.

You may have to do some legwork to get your book into the right places for sale. In the context of a business book, for example, it may not be relevant to get your book into the local bookstore but it may be useful to have it featured in the business college bookshop. You need to think about who is going to read your book and where those people are likely to be. A growing number of people, especially those searching for specialist titles, search online. Online retailers such as Amazon are fast become *the* place to shop if you need a book – especially a specialist non-fiction book.

Who Is Best Suited to Print-On-Demand Publishing?

I believe that print-on-demand has many great advantages and really changes the game for authors and publishers alike. Print-on-demand is best suited to you if:

- You want their book quickly, say for an upcoming conference or event.

- You have the content to create good books but don't necessarily have natural markets to sell to. POD provides a built-in selling channel.

- You want to have a book but are conscious of your environmental footprint and don't want to print thousands on the off-chance you can sell them.

- You can't get a traditional publisher interested but are still very confident in your product. There is a caveat to this however – think *X Factor* contestants here. For those unfamiliar with *X Factor*, it's a TV show where everyday people audition for singing stardom. Some people who audition are truly brilliant and some are not! Sometimes confidence is seriously misplaced, or borderline delusional! Be sure to seek external opinion from people who know your market before you go investing in something that may just end up breaking your heart.

- You want to get really clever and target your book to particular niche groups and tailor-make content based on the audience.

A Passing Word on Vanity Publishing

POD is not vanity publishing. Vanity publishing is just what it says it is! A publisher will wax lyrical about the quality of your manuscript and soothe your ego. They will then explain the process which will include *you* paying *them* a significant amount of money to produce your book. In essence vanity publishers are little more than book printers.

There is nothing to be gained from this route at all. It's expensive and the quality or saleability of the book is unimportant to the publisher. The vanity publisher doesn't care if you want to publish the *History of the Paperclip*. All they care about is parting you from your cash and making you feel important.

If you have a natural market and are confident that you can sell a significant number of books then either negotiate a proper contract with a traditional publisher, seek a publishing partnership agreement with a traditional publisher or better still use print-on-demand technology. It's cheaper, the quality is the same or better and your book automatically plugs into a sales and distribution system. That doesn't happen in vanity publishing.

Even if you have buckets of cash and a pet project which doesn't necessarily have any commercial merit for either you or a publisher there is always a better alternative to vanity publishing.

Summary of Key Points

- Print-on-demand is the most exciting thing to happen to authors since the Biro or the memory stick!

- So what is print-on-demand? Exactly what it says it is. The book will only be printed when there is a demand for it.

- When someone finds your book and orders it, the POD company processes the payment, prints the book and delivers it to the customer. You pay for the printing cost but only for the books that are sold and you receive a royalty on the sale.

- In addition if you want a quantity of your own books for promotional purposes or to sell to your existing contacts or at seminars and events you simply pay the cost price of printing and delivery. That way you can enjoy an even higher margin on books you sell yourself.

- There are a number of POD companies out there – the big ones are CreateSpace (formerly known as BookSurge) and Lightening Source Incorporated (LSI).

- There are significant advantages of print-on-demand that make it superior to self-publishing. The main advantages are low set-up costs, flexibility, access to sales channels, and POD is environmentally friendly, fast and credible.

- All you need to do is supply the POD company with your book and pay a fee. The size of that fee depends on how much you want the POD company to do and how much you have done yourself.

- Regardless of how you choose to upload the files or what services you choose from your POD company, it's much less expensive than self-publishing. There is no major investment required as you only pay for printing when the book is ordered.

- If something in your book suddenly changes, for example advice you give is no longer accurate because of changing legislation, then you can just change the files.

- A great POD company will get your book listed with all the major distributors and booksellers so the sales problem of self-publishing is at least partially overcome.

- Selling the book is probably the hardest part, so having this done for you is a *major* benefit.

- POD is much more environmentally friendly than printing thousands of books that you *hope* you'll sell.

- You could have a physical book in your hand within weeks of finishing the manuscript. Compare that to the traditional publishing model and it's a clear winner.

- There are very few *real* disadvantages of print-on-demand but the sceptics will tell you that the main disadvantages are lower profit margin, possible contract issues and reputation question marks.

- Print-on-demand companies effectively do everything a traditional publisher does except marketing and yet you will receive about 35 percent in royalty as opposed to 10 – 15 percent.

- Some contracts can be restrictive, so make sure you read the contract thoroughly, ask for clarification on issues you're unclear of, and never be afraid to negotiate.

- Questions have been raised about POD's reputation – but again I don't believe this is valid. Most people wouldn't even be able to tell the difference between a POD book and a book published by a major publisher.

- Print-on-demand is certainly the most exciting thing to happen to publishing for a long time and it finally offers authors a legitimate avenue to get a professional-looking physical product without selling their soul to get it.

- Print-on-demand is best suited to you if you want your book quickly and have the content to create good books but don't necessarily have natural markets to sell to. POD provides a built-in selling channel. It is also suited to your if you want to have a book but are conscious of your environmental footprint or you can't get a traditional publisher interested, or if you want to get really clever and target your book to particular niche groups and tailor-make content based on the audience.

- POD is not vanity publishing. Vanity publishing is just what it says it is! A publisher will wax lyrical about the quality of your manuscript and soothe your ego.

- If you have a natural market and are confident that you can sell a significant number of books then either negotiate a proper contract with a traditional publisher or use print-on-demand technology. It's cheaper, the quality is the same or better and your book automatically plugs into a sales and distribution system. That doesn't happen in vanity publishing.

Chapter 17
The New Way – E-Books

If you are creating and selling information,
you'll never go out of business.
~ Michael LeBoeuf

E-books were initially touted as the next big thing in publishing and predictions were made about the end of the physical book. That hasn't happened and it's unlikely it ever will but e-books are now available in a variety of formats and their popularity is growing all the time. In 2010 Amazon reported that e-book sales had outsold hardcover sales for the first time.

In the same way that digital music changed the music industry e-books are changing the publishing industry. And the battle lines are drawn around the device and format.

Although there are many specific e-readers such as Amazon's Kindle, Sony Reader, Barnes & Noble Nook and Kobo, these devices also compete with almost every tablet computer which doubles as a reading device.

Although industry speculation pits the Amazon Kindle in the blue corner and the Apple iPad in the red corner it may not end up being quite so straightforward. Although there is no doubt that Apple want to do for book publishing what iTunes did for music publishing both Apple and Amazon have access to a massive sales platform. But the products are *very* different and consequently it's unlikely that it will be a simple either/or battle.

The Kindle is a dedicated reader with access to Amazon. It is inexpensive, light and has a massive battery life. It uses the most advanced e-ink technology which makes reading from a Kindle very similar to reading from a physical book. That means you can read a Kindle for a long time without getting a headache and you can read it easily outside or in the sunshine – just like a book.

The Apple iPad is not just a reading device – it's a tablet and consequently it's considerably more expensive. The books from iTunes or iBookstore are beautiful. The visual experience is far superior to the Kindle but then there is no visual experience when you are actually reading a book. It's usually black and white text on a page. Reading an e-book from the iPad may be a really sumptuous experience and you may love using the touch screen to flick the pages over but it's not something you will probably be comfortable doing for long. And that's the big difference. If you want to review full colour books which have beautiful design, or read a bedtime story with your child, then the iPad is stunning. But if you want to read the latest novel at the beach then the Kindle is the clear winner. It's likely therefore that many people will end up owning both and will use them differently for different books and different activities.

As for the format, there are two main formats – Mobi and ePub. Amazon's Kindle uses its own proprietary format based on Mobi called AZW. This means that anyone who wants to sell their e-book in Kindle format to be sold through Amazon must convert the file to the Kindle format. Most other e-readers and tablets use some form of ePub. EPub is more flexible and offers more design features.

Personally, I've always believed that e-books have huge potential. But that potential was not just about having an electronic version of a book. The additional opportunity of e-books is the opportunity to bring the written word to life. Many of the e-reader options already allow you to search the text and add notes to your electronic books but much more is possible.

This book has had many previous lives. First I created it in PDF format which was the e-book format of choice a few years ago. PDF is still widely used because all devices read PDF and it's not platform specific. Then I discovered a format called DNL which is utterly brilliant software. The pages "turned" like a real book and it allowed me to incorporate a variety of multimedia options. With DNL you can add sound, voice files, music, and flash graphics (excellent for making graphs and diagrams come to life). You can embed video or even "stream" it from a website to the book so that every time the reader opens the book, new updated video or audio appears in their copy. The application for that in training material is endless! DNL also has a built in search function and allows you to highlight text and add notes into the book. You can create interactive quizzes, surveys and tests which readers can complete and get the answers immediately. But DNL didn't have a big enough sales platform and that's why Amazon and/or Apple are likely to be the eventual winners in the e-publishing space.

The good news for authors is that e-publishing is changing the face of publishing forever and there is no reason why you wouldn't make your e-book available in all formats for all devices. Having a physical book is still superior for the kudos of being an author and is always preferable as a business development tool. But e-books extend your reach and will probably appeal to a different audience. You're just giving your would-be reader as many options to buy your book as possible.

Advantages of E-Books

There are several significant advantages of e-books and those advantages are likely to increase over time. Whilst not for everyone and not for every book, the advantages of e-books are:

- Speed to Market

- Larger Margins

- Instant Delivery

- Powerful Marketing Tool

- Get Traditional Publishers' Attention

Speed to Market

If you are smart then regardless of how you choose to distribute your book you will have gone through a thorough pre-production process involving a professional editor, copy-editor proofreader, designer, typesetter and indexer. The beauty of e-publishing, however, is that once that crucial stage is complete it takes minutes to get that finished file to market. With e-publishing that finished file is simply converted to the necessary format and uploaded to the various distribution networks and it's ready to purchase and download. With a physical product you will need to wait while the printer creates the physical book.

As I said earlier I used BookPOD (www.bookpod.com.au) to sort everything out for me. I provided a Word file and they typeset the book and uploaded the file to CreateSpace for the POD physical product via Amazon whilst also converting that file to Mobi and ePub formats so that this book was available as an e-book available through Amazon (Kindle), iTunes, iBookstore, Barnes and Noble, Bookworld, Angus & Robertson, and Ingram.

Whatever format you choose, and whether you choose to do this process yourself or get someone to help, once the pre-production is complete, your book can be online ready for sale within a matter of minutes.

Larger Margins

Because the book is never printed (unless by the customer) there are very few up-front production costs and no inventory to store. As a result, e-publishing offers the potential for greater profit. However, this very much depends on the format you choose.

If you create your own e-book using PDF or another format and sell that product through your own marketing, database or website then you have control over what you sell your product for. And in this situation there definitely is a greater capacity for profit. Certainly I have read of many people who have set out to write a book and instead chose to turn each chapter into a special report selling successfully for US$10 each. If a book has 10 to 15 chapters you can see why this is a profitable way to publish! Online shoppers are scouring the Internet for specific information and if you are providing it through an e-book that is delivered to their inbox instantly, they will pay for that.

But this is only relevant when you are selling your product yourself. If you want to tap into the sales channels of Amazon or Apple there is less flexibility. With Amazon, for example, they want to sell volume so they offer significantly greater royalty on books priced competitively. You can still charge more for your book but if you do, the royalty percentage is much smaller. Basically, when you plug into the various sales channels you will have to choose from that sales channel's options and those options will dictate how much you make in royalty. When you are ready to publish you will need to check what those options are at the time and decide the best course of action for your product.

Instant Delivery

Online shoppers are incredibly impatient and when they are on a quest to find something they invariably want immediate access to it. This drive for instant gratification is certainly helping to legitimise e-publishing as a valid and necessary part of your overall distribution strategy.

This is especially true of information products or "how to" products, where the searcher is often engaged in the task and will hop online to find solutions to problems as they present themselves.

Many of the e-reader devices have WiFi which means that someone can go online with their reader or tablet and buy the book they want and it will be available within a matter of seconds.

Powerful Marketing Tool

Information products such as e-books or special reports offer a very cost-effective promotional tool to add value to your product or service offering. They have a high perceived value and can be a very effective way to gather a warm list of potential customers and keeping existing customers happy and loyal.

Books, either e-books or physical books, act as a very low entry point to your product range or service offer and allow would-be customers to sample your professionalism, skill and knowledge without having to make a major investment. E-products offer an affordable promotional device that can get prospective clients in the door.

An e-book can create a buzz about your personal brand or product and they have been used very effectively by some very smart people. In 2000, Seth Godin wrote his third book, an e-book called *Unleashing The Ideavirus*, which was free to download as PDF. He also encouraged people to send it on to friends. As a result, it was a living demonstration of his book's topic – how fast an idea can spread around the world using modern technology and some creativity. The book is said to be the most popular e-book ever written and established Godin as a marketing legend.

Get Traditional Publishers' Attention

Seth Godin's marketing genius also resulted in his e-book being translated into ten languages and published in both hardcover and paperback. The buzz he created with the book caught the attention of traditional publishing.

His experience is not unique. Many of the books that you can buy in your local bookshop started life as an e-book or a self-published book. An author called Michael Meanwell wrote an e-book called the *Enterprising Writer* and also wrote a special bonus book called *Writers on Writing,* which buyers received if they bought his first e-book. The book sold steadily online and attracted the attention of a mainstream publisher and Meanwell is now a published author in the traditional sense of the word.

E-books allow you to get to market quickly, test your product cost-effectively, improve on the idea and make some money too. All of this is then field experience and evidence that can be used to attract the interest of a mainstream publisher if that is what you ultimately want. It also demonstrates to publishers that you are prepared to trust your ideas and back them with your own time, money and energy.

Disadvantages of E-Books

E-books used to be a little like the gold rush days. In the early days they were only created as Word files or PDF and like the gold rush they attracted the attention of the "Get-Rich-Quick-Brigade". Plagiarism was rife, writing was poor and they would be pitched as "insider secrets" often selling for significantly more than a traditional book. They were almost always disappointing and as a result e-books got a bad reputation. But the advent of the Amazon Kindle and iPad etc. has changed people's perception of e-books and now the only genuine disadvantage is:

• Less Clout Than a Physical Book

Less Clout Than a Physical Book

In comparison to all the hoops you have to jump through to secure a publishing contract and the time it takes to see your book on the shelf, creating an e-book is a walk in the park. Yet human beings believe that if something is hard work or takes a long time to do, then it's got more intrinsic value. As a result, e-books are their physical counterpart's poor cousin. But even that is changing...

Seth Godin certainly improved the image of e-publishing. Bestselling author Stephen King has also done a great deal to legitimise the medium. In 2000 he posted his novella, *Riding the Bullet,* on the Internet and 500,000 copies were downloaded in 48 hours. As a consequence, submissions to e-publishers quadrupled and sales of e-books tripled. It was a clear warning shot across the traditional publishers' respective bows and King's actions – while mainly a publicity stunt – also gave e-publishing instant legitimacy. After all, if e-publishing was good enough for a literary legend like Stephen King, then perhaps it's good enough for you and me!

If you are writing your book for the status it will give you as an expert in your field then ultimately you should aim to have your book published in physical form. There are, however, exceptions such as if your business is in the innovation, technology or Internet arena. For example, Seth Godin's e-book worked so well because it demonstrated the power of his ideas. His free e-book was itself an "Ideavirus" rather than just being a document about an Ideavirus. With the help of the Internet it spread around the globe in a flash and made Seth Godin famous.

E-books most definitely have their place in publishing so don't dismiss them out of hand. They can offer a very valid revenue stream and can further establish you as a thought leader and innovator in your field. Make sure you make an outstanding product and you can reap the rewards of e-publishing.

E-Book Production Checklist

Don't cut corners. That means going through the same process as you would to write a physical book.

- Make sure it's the best it can be, get it professionally edited, copy-edited and proofread.

- Get a designer to create a cover, including title, author and website link.

- Have it professionally laid out and designed.

- Apply for an ISBN and include the copyright information.

- Ensure that the contents page is automatically generated so that each section is clickable so the reader can easily find their chosen topic.

- Include an author bio, list of additional products, order form and links to your website and social media platforms.

Who Is Best Suited to E-Publishing?

There are considerable additional advantages to e-books that you need to consider in the wider context of what you are trying to achieve. E-publishing will be especially useful if:

- Your book is time specific, meaning that creating a physical product would be pointless. For example, a how-to e-book on technology would be particularly useful, as the e-book can be easily updated and kept fresh and relevant as the technology evolves and the instructions change.

- You can make a better impact with speed rather than by sending a hard copy book. For example, you could email your e-book to a potential client immediately. That speed of response is impressive in modern business. A book would take a few days to reach that client.

- You want to create a book cost-effectively. E-publishing still has costs (see checklist above) but it's still cheaper than publishing a physical product.

- You want to get your ideas to market within weeks, not months or years.

- You are having trouble finding a mainstream publisher. Publish online initially and use sales figures to prove your product has a market.

- You want to test your material and finetune the book, while potentially also making a little cash up front.

- Your business is content-rich and you are keen to experiment with online publishing to create a bank of information products that your business can give away to clients as value-add loyalty building products, or sell as additional revenue streams.

Summary of Key Points

- E-books were initially touted as the next big thing in publishing and predictions were made about the end of the physical book. That hasn't happened and it's unlikely it ever will, but e-books are now available in a variety of formats and their popularity is growing all the time.

- In the same way that digital music changed the music industry e-books are changing the publishing industry. And the battle lines are drawn around the device and format.

- Personally, I've always believed that e-books have huge potential. But that potential was not just about having an electronic version of a book. The additional opportunity of e-books is the opportunity to bring the written word to life. Many of the e-reader options already allow you to search the text and add notes to your electronic books but much more is possible.

- The good news for authors is that e-publishing is changing the face of publishing forever and there is no reason why you wouldn't make your e-book available in all formats for all devices.

- Whilst not for everyone and not for every book the advantages of e-books are speed to market, larger margins, instant delivery, a powerful marketing tool, and a successful e-book can help attract the attention of a traditional publisher.

- Once the pre-production is complete your book can be online ready for sale within a matter of minutes.

- Because the book is never printed (unless by the customer) there are very few up-front production costs and no inventory to store. As a result, e-publishing offers the potential for greater profit.

- Online shoppers are incredibly impatient and when they are on a quest to find something they invariably want immediate access to it. This drive for instant gratification is certainly helping to legitimise e-publishing as a valid and necessary part of your overall distribution strategy.

- Information products such as e-books or special reports offer a very cost-effective promotional tool to add value to your product or service offering.

- E-books allow you to get to market quickly, test your product cost-effectively, improve on the idea and make some money too. All of this is then field experience and evidence that can be used to attract the interest of a mainstream publisher if that is what you ultimately want.

- With the advent of the Amazon Kindle and iPad, people's perception of e-books has now changed and the only genuine disadvantage is that they have less clout than a physical book.

- If you are writing your book for the status it will give you as an expert in your field then ultimately you should aim to have your book published in physical form.

- E-books most definitely have their place in publishing so don't dismiss them out of hand. They can offer a very valid revenue stream and can further establish you as a thought leader and innovator in your field. Make sure you make an outstanding product and you can reap the rewards of e-publishing.

- Don't cut corners. That means going through the same process as you would to write a physical book.

- E-publishing will be especially useful if your book is time specific, or will need to be updated regularly, and if you want to create a book cost-effectively and you want to get your ideas to market within weeks, not months or years. It's also a viable option if you are having trouble finding a mainstream publisher or if you want to test your material and finetune the book, and your business is content- rich and you are keen to experiment with e-publishing to create a bank of information products.

Chapter 18

What's the Right Publishing Strategy?

A good book, in the language of the book-sellers, is a
saleable one; in that of the curious, a scarce one; in
that of men of sense, a useful and instructive one.
~ Oswald Chambers

In order to work out what the right publishing strategy is you need to think about your intentions and objectives for the book and how best to meet those often-competing priorities.

For example, when I wrote this book I had several reasons and objectives...

- As a professional writer I have seen time and again just how powerful a book can be as a brand and business development tool. It offers a considerable competitive advantage and I wanted to let people know that.

- I wanted to inspire readers to write the book they've been talking about for years and help them see that, with a little planning, it is possible.

- Not everyone can afford to hire a ghostwriter or wants to hire a ghostwriter but often they don't know where to start. I wanted to help those people.

- I also wanted this book to be an advertisement for my ability as a writer so that should a reader love the idea of writing a book but decide they really didn't have the time, skill or desire to write their own, they would consider contacting me. I wanted to "walk my talk" and create a "live" demonstration of the business development tool I'm advocating.

- I am also keen to experiment with the new publishing options available – especially POD and e-publishing. I'm interested to find out if these new forms of publishing really do herald a new dawn for authors or is it simply a changing of the guard.

Initially I chose to create an e-book first to test what happened and frankly not much did. I was optimistic after an early flurry of sales but in the end it was a good reminder that no matter who or what publishes your book *you* need to sell it yourself and spend time finding ways to sell it. I didn't do that because I was busy writing books.

Even if your book is great you must accept the responsibility for promoting it. And that is true whether you secure a mainstream publishing contract or go it alone. The best way to sell books is face to face at events or speaking engagements. It's certainly the best way to sell books in big numbers. If these sorts of opportunities present themselves to you as an author – take them. If they don't present themselves then hunt them down. Speak to audiences without charge if you have to and simply sell your book at the back of the room.

Think about who will read your book or who you want to read your book and think about what else those people are doing? Where do they go? How do they spend their time? Getting your book in a bookshop or listing it on Amazon is not the end point in terms of your marketing and promotion involvement. It is the starting point. If you really want to sell your book in volume you need to get active and stay active. It's worth pointing out that according to statistics from the publishing industry 68 percent of all books are bought by women. Fifty-two percent of all books are not sold in bookshops. Instead they are merchandised through book clubs and non-traditional retail outlets. So think about what else your target market might be buying and place your book in those places. If your book is on exotic plants, for example, you could seek to have your book stocked in Garden Centres or DIY outlets. And for the record 64 percent of book buyers couldn't care less whether the book is in a bestseller list or not.

If you would like more information on how best to promote your book for maximum sales Brian Jud has written a great book called *Beyond the Bookstore: How to sell more books profitably to non bookstore markets.*

To sell in any real volume you first need to make your book as widely available as possible so that the most number of people have access to it. As much as I loved the DNL version and the cool features that it offered it became clear that people didn't want to learn a new format and they didn't necessarily want to download another bit of software prior to buying the book so they could read it. As a consequence of this learning I have now revised the book, updating the information where necessary to create a second edition. The publishing industry has moved on still further since the first DNL e-book version and this book is now available in a variety of different formats including physical POD and more popular e-book formats including Kindle thus ensuring the widest possible reach.

For your own situation, you will have to think about what you are trying to achieve with your book, the industry you are in and your long-term business objectives. Below is a reminder of the main benefits and what type of publishing hits the mark for each.

Priority	Traditional Publishing	Self Publishing	Print on Demand	E-publishing
Fast to market	✗	?	✓	✓
Revenue potential	✗	?	✓	✓
Credibility	✓	?	✓	?
Guarantee publication	✗	✓	✓	✓
Prefer minimum post writing involvement	✓	✗	✗	✗

If speed to market is key then POD and/or e-publishing is for you.

If credibility is critical then persevere until you secure a traditional publishing contract from a well-known imprint (which is not easy) or self-publish using POD. Credibility will be assumed with POD so long as the book looks fantastic, is professionally produced and the publisher is not listed as a name too close to your name or business name. For example, this book is published by Word Architect Publishing – my business name is Word Architect as is my website so this book is obviously self-published. I did this deliberately to show potential clients that I could write and publish their book but this is not a wise move under any other circumstances. In most cases making the publishing name close to your own business name is a mistake as it makes it obvious that the book is self-published, so use a different name. In other words if your business is called *Sundial Consulting* don't publish your book under Sundial Publishing! The fact is that most people wouldn't have a clue whether something was published or self-published just by looking at the name of the publisher.

For example, if you picked up a book and it was published by Piatkus, would you think it better or more credible than a book published by Peachpit Press or Quixotic? Chances are you wouldn't have a clue and you probably wouldn't care so long as the book looked professional and contained good information. Most authors want their book to have credibility but most people can't tell a self-published book from a traditionally published book unless you get a major imprint like John Wiley & Sons or Harper Collins. For the record Piatkus is owned by Little, Brown Book group which is part of Holtzbrinck Publishing Holdings – one of the largest traditional publishers in the world. Peachpit Press is an imprint of Pearson – another traditional publishing giant. And finally Quixotic is a great word but as far as I know it is not the name of a publishing company – I made it up.

If you want your book to appear in high street bookshops or airport bookshops then you really need to secure a traditional publishing contract. It is possible to visit bookshops and tout your book direct but few people have the inclination and fewer still are accepted. And it's impossible to approach airport booksellers direct. Getting your book into airports is a dark art that requires a traditional publisher. Having said that, just because you get a traditional publishing contract does not mean you will automatically get into high street shops or airports.

If you absolutely want a book then the only guarantee is self-publishing, print-on-demand or e-publishing. If you don't want to get involved in the minutia of detail required to get this right then employ someone from an author services company such as BookPOD (www.bookpod.com.au) to manage everything for you.

It's also worth noting that it doesn't really matter what publishing option you choose if your book is rubbish! Being able to call yourself an author will always open doors but if the book is poorly written or badly produced then it's not going to do you any favours in the long run.

And by bad, I don't just mean poor content, spelling errors and poor paper quality. For a book to yield its business development promise you need to write it with your marketing hat on. If you do, a well written engaging book will act as the ultimate business card and your silent salesman. It will do more to establish your credibility than hundreds of phone calls and thousands of sales letters. So be vigilant and make sure you avoid the 7 Fatal Book Writing Mistakes.

The 7 Fatal Book Writing Flaws

There are several ways to massively reduce the effectiveness of your book and each one will take you one step closer to publishing oblivion.

1. **Getting on your soap box.** Writing a book is an opportunity to showcase your knowledge and expertise, it's not an opportunity to get on your soap box. Readers are only interested in how you can benefit *them* so stay focused on the reader and don't get on your soap box.

2. **Using overly formal language.** Traditionally business writing is often formal, dull and usually passive. This may be okay for a business memo but it makes for a very dry and boring book. You need to bring the material to life with real life examples and case studies that illustrate

your ability to solve a particular problem. Be conversational and engaging so you draw the reader in and don't be afraid to use humour where appropriate.

3. **Not enough substance.** You need to be precise, detailed and complete in your explanation of your idea, methodology or solution. The reader is looking for information that will help them in their situation so give it to them. Don't hold back. When you offer genuine insight and value then the reader will develop trust and faith in your expertise and is therefore more likely to recruit you to help them solve their challenges. Don't pad your book out with fluff.

4. **Being too vague.** Providing weak general examples instead of real specific examples creates sloppy, poor quality writing. When writing your book you may be tempted to write to a broad audience. As a result, you try to be all things to all people and end up being nothing to no one. Focus on your target market.

5. **Including too much opinion.** Your opinion may be interesting but it's always stronger when you can back it up by research or other verifiable third party evidence. Wherever possible stick to the facts and never criticise a competitor.

6. **Weak or no marketing focus.** A book is like any other product or service – you can publish and be damned if you like but unless you have established if there is a genuine market for your message, you may end up very disappointed.

7. **Too many production errors.** Nothing, not even a brilliantly written book will make up for poor design, bad layout and spelling mistakes. Most people will forgive one or two in a standard book but any more than that and you've shot yourself in the foot. If you self-publish, then you must follow due process and involve the necessary professionals to deliver a product that is indistinguishable from a mainstream publisher.

I have met a few people over the years who have poured their heart and soul into writing a book with high expectations of how it will transform their career. For most it has genuinely delivered on that objective, albeit not through royalty income or in a way they originally envisaged. There are however exceptions. I remember being given a copy of one book where the author was very excited and optimistic about his future. I looked at the book but sadly didn't share his enthusiasm. Of course, I didn't say anything. The book was complete so there was nothing my pessimism would add to the process. I heard a couple of years later that the author had struggled to sell a few meagre copies and it had not given his career the boost he expected.

I wasn't surprised because the author had incorporated almost all the fatal flaws. The book itself wasn't badly written, it had some good information, it even had a nice hook. But as a business development tool it bombed because it didn't show how the author could help the reader and how he could make a positive impact on their life. It didn't solve any pressing problems the reader might face and it certainly didn't use case studies or examples to illustrate how the author was an expert in his field. It was generic and woolly and as a result it lacked power and influence. In short, it didn't showcase his business in any way; it was really just a nice piece of personal philosophy. Remember the figures from earlier where some 86,000 new titles were available in the UK in 2007 and just over 58,000 sold an average of 18 copies. You don't want to be selling 18 copies so make sure the book solves a problem that your clients or customers have.

You have to remember the old marketing platitude WIIFM – tune into station "What's In It For Me". Human beings are inherently selfish. We are searching for things that will make a difference, solve a specific problem, or otherwise help us to create more love, money, health, success, happiness or enjoyment.

If you and your business can do that – then spell it out and showcase your success in achieving those goals for other people. And make sure you deliver on each and every promise you make.

Summary of Key Points

- Knowing your options is important because it will influence your ideal publishing strategy. You need to think about your intentions and objectives for the book and how best to meet those often-competing priorities.

- If speed to market is key then POD and/or e-publishing is for you.

- If credibility is critical then either source a traditional publishing contract from a well-known and well recognised imprint (which is extremely hard) or self-publish using POD.

- Credibility will be assumed with POD so long as the book looks fantastic, is professionally produced and the publisher is not listed as a name too close to your name or business name.

- If you want your book to appear in high street bookshops or airport bookshops then you really need to secure a traditional publishing contract.

- It is possible to visit bookshops and tout your book direct but few people have the inclination and fewer still are accepted.

- It's impossible to approach airport booksellers direct. Getting your book into airports is a dark art that requires a traditional publisher.

- Having said that, just because you get a traditional publishing contract does not mean you will automatically get into high street shops or airports.

- If you absolutely want a book then the only guarantee is self-publishing via POD or e-publishing and if you don't want to get involved with the work after the writing then hire a company like BookPOD (www.bookpod.com.au) to manage everything for you.

- It's also worth noting that it doesn't really matter what publishing option you choose if your book is rubbish! Being able to call yourself an author will always open doors but if the book is poorly written or badly produced then it's not going to do you any favours in the long run.

- There are several ways to massively reduce the effectiveness of your book and each one will take you one step closer to publishing failure. So if you want to guarantee publishing failure then get on your soap box, write in the same style as you'd write a business letter or memo, talk about yourself instead of talking about your idea, methodology or solution, write about vague generalities instead of specific examples, fill your book with fluff, ignore marketing principles and create an amateur-looking book.

- You have to remember the old marketing platitude WIIFM – tune into station "What's In It For Me". Human beings are inherently selfish. We are searching for things that will make a difference, solve a specific problem, or otherwise help us to create more love, money, health, success, happiness or enjoyment.

- If you and your business can do that – then spell it out and showcase your success in achieving those goals. And make sure you deliver on each and every promise you make.

Conclusion

It's difficult to say with any real certainty why being an author is such a powerful business tool. Perhaps it's because in school we were taught to revere books and there was an unspoken assumption that if something was written in a book it must be true.

I think this long-standing reverence for books is certainly part of the puzzle. Books continue to hold a strong fascination for people. Business people still use an extensive library to impress their visitors while they wait in boardrooms. The repertoire usually consists of timeless classics such as *Think and Grow Rich, Build to Last, Seven Habits of Highly Effective People, The Art of War, In Search of Excellence* etc. The fact that their little spines haven't been tickled in years doesn't seem to matter although reading them would also be beneficial! The sad reality is that according to publishing industry statistics most readers will not get past page 18 of a book they have purchased. That's staggering and, for a professional writer like me, more than a little depressing, but it doesn't alter the fact that having a great book can really turbo-charge your career and business impact.

There is something special about a book, and to paraphrase Mark Twain: reports of their death have been greatly exaggerated. Despite the Internet revolution, the physical book business is still alive and well. Why? Because there is something magical about a book, it's personal, portable and accessible and there is something much more enjoyable, almost spiritual, about reading a book as opposed to reading from a computer screen or gadget.

To me the screen versus paper argument is a lot like the cork versus screw top argument for wine. Screw top may be convenient and it may ensure the quality of the wine but something is lost in the experience nonetheless. As part of the wine drinking experience, cork is wholly superior – if nothing else but for the sound it makes and the intangible sensations of celebration and anticipation. A screw top may indeed be more functional and deliver greater consistency of quality but there is no emotion – it just doesn't feel the same. It's the same with a physical book.

A digital e-book reader or tablet may indeed have some advantages, not least the saving of natural resources, but the experience of reading is entirely different. Functionality and speed are not the only important considerations in life and they never will be. Books are so much more than the sum of their parts.

There is also something courageous about books. Pouring your heart and soul into a book and sending it out into the world for appraisal can be a terrifying prospect. I have experienced this myself and also with clients who get to the final stage of a book and freeze. There is always some urgent business agenda that takes precedence over the completion of the book, even if it's written for them and the "author" just has to read it!

There is something genuinely scary about drawing a line in the sand and saying, "This is what I believe. This is my truth." As an author you have to take a stand for your ideas and be willing to let them go. You also have to be willing to accept that you may look back and cringe at those same ideas (although if you do, you just write a second edition!). Life is never static, we change and our ideas and attitudes change, and yet once a book is "out there" it is a permanent reminder of a moment in time. As a result, writing a book can require courage. Perhaps that's part of the reason we respect authors so much!

In the end, it doesn't really matter *why* we respect authors – all that matters is that we do (maybe that's why we refer to author-ity). You can witness a tangible shift in respect, admiration and trust between two people when one has just found out the other has written a book – even if it was years ago!

Being an author has impact. We all understand the importance of looking the part, even if you are a one-man-band working out of an Internet cafe in Bogota. You have to be able to deliver on your promises and consistently provide more than expected. But in order to do that you have to get into a position where people will trust you enough to hire your business or buy your product or service in the first place.

And that has always been the tricky bit. How do you stand out from the competition? How do you compete with the thousands of advertising messages vying for your customers' attention? How do you increase your fees in an economic downturn? How do you create additional revenue or open up new markets? How do you reach a wider audience?

Despite the endless questions, there is only one solution that meets all these objectives and more...

• Write a book!

Being good enough is no longer good enough. You have to sell yourself in the face of global competition and that means differentiating yourself and your business through the presentation and formalisation of your intellectual property.

A book offers you an opportunity, not only to position yourself as the expert you are, and deliver insightful and useful information to an eager audience, but also, if written correctly, it is a long copy sales device that is never thrown away!

Books build trust and respect – two vital ingredients in any business relationship. If you believe in the value you provide and have plenty of happy clients to prove it then writing a book can act as a powerful way to build your reputation, client base and income.

Time is the most precious resource we have and time is often the very thing that stops aspiring authors from achieving their goal, especially when those aspiring authors also have a business to run. But if you consider the age-old ratio touted by Pareto then you really can't afford NOT to write a book. If 20 percent of your activity accounts for 80 percent of your income, you can be sure that writing a book is a 20 percent activity.

Being a published author will do more for your credibility, authority and profitability than any other single marketing initiative – often at a fraction of the cost. It will get you free publicity, open up speaking opportunities if you want them, and create new revenue streams and future product development opportunities. It will allow you to pick and choose your clients and increase your fees.

And if you really don't feel you have the time, patience or skill to write your own book then maybe it's time to hire a writer. To contact me visit my website www.wordarchitect.com.

Remember...

> *Without books the development of*
> *civilization would have been impossible.*
> *They are the engines of change, windows on*
> *the world, "Lighthouses", as the poet said,*
> *"erected in the sea of time." They are companions,*
> *teachers, magicians, bankers of the treasures*
> *of the mind. Books are humanity in print.*
> *~ Arthur Schopenhauer*

Good luck.

Index

A

Amazon 3, 203, 211, 220, 222, 223, 232
Amazon's POD division. *See* CreateSpace
Angus & Robertson 223
Apple 18, 66, 220, 221, 223
Association of American Publishers (APP) 3
Attenborough, David 7
authors
  doors open for 7
  others' perception of 15
  respect for 242–243

B

bestseller, no formula for 179, 191–193
Bettger, Frank 47, 78
B-format book. *See* book formats: B-format
book
  death of 3, 219, 241
  power of 6
  reverence for 241
  sales figures and statistics 27, 180, 184, 232, 233
  versus e-book 3, 242
book dimensions. *See* book formats

book formats
  B-format 102
  Demy 102
BookPOD 209, 222, 235
BookStatistics.com 154, 189
BookSurge. *See* CreateSpace
book, writing and having one
  as business card 6, 27, 174
  as business development tool 6, 54, 104, 237
  as marketing tool 7, 104
  differentiating you from competition 6, 16
  establishing you as expert 5, 16, 32, 41–42, 44
  increasing influence 16
  increasing your business sales 31–40
  increasing your income 26
  increasing your profile 16, 39
  real value of 27
  return on investment 33
  selling and promoting your book 232
  suitability of as marketing strategy 63–64, 65
  timing of as marketing strategy 67–68
book writing problems
  lacking ability to write 144–145
  lacking desire to write 143

lacking time to write 145
7 fatal book writing flaws 235–236
book writing process
  brain dump 96–97
  central premise, staying focused on
    92–93, 95, 105
  content, creating 95–100
  cover design 138–139
  editing stage. See editing
  heading hierarchy 98–100
  idea clusters, ordering 97–98
  length of book 102–104
  mind map, creating 96
  planning of book 74, 91–92
  recognising how you work best
    76–78, 87
  structure 100–101
  structure, importance of 73–74,
    91–92
  Table of Contents, generating 98–100,
    105, 106–107
  title or working title 93–95, 101, 105,
    106
  title, self-explanatory 93, 94
book writing process, marketing per-
    spective 78–86
  clarifying your intention for book
    74–76
  communicating benefits not features
    85–89
  knowing your target market 79–81,
    101
  solving problems of ideal client 82–83
  targeting good clients 81–82
  title hook or gimmick 93–94, 101,
    105, 106
  Unique Selling Proposition (USP),
    knowing your 84–85, 89
brand/branding
  brand war, Microsoft and Apple 18
  creating a conditioned response
    20–22
  creating relationships 17–20

description of 14
developing your 11–25
differentiating yourself from competi-
    tion 15–17, 38
importance of perception 11–13
improving your 4
Bryson, Bill 58
Burgess, Paul 46, 76, 131
business card, book as. See book, writ-
    ing and having one: as business
    card
Business Coaching Systems (BCS) 35
business development tool. See book,
    writing and having one: as busi-
    ness development tool
business sales, closing more 34–38

C

career, diversifying and expanding
    51–55
  consulting 51
  seminars and speaking. See speaking
    engagements and seminars
  training 51
Cialdini, Robert 14, 16, 18, 23–25, 33,
    36, 40, 42, 81
Cialdini's six principles of influence
  commitment or consistency 14–15
  law of reciprocity 33–34, 39
  liking someone 18
  respect for authority 16–17
  scarcity 42
  social proof 36, 81
client base, generating more desirable 5
client relationships, strengthening of 38
clients
  and jobs, having choice of 43
  generating more 5
Coca-Cola 5, 13, 15, 22, 66
conscious competence learning matrix
    155–156
copy-editing 199. See also editing
five Cs 177

importance of 177–178
Covey, Stephen 101, 102
CreateSpace 208
Cummings, E. E. 191

D
Darwin, Charles 58
deals
  closing more 5
death of the book. *See* book: death of
Demy book format. *See* book formats: Demy
developing your brand. *See* brand/branding: developing your
Dubner, Stephen J. 102

E
e-book formats
  DNL 221
  PDF 221
e-books
  huge potential of 221
  production of, checklist 227
  versus printed books 3
  who best suited to 227
e-books, advantages of 222
  few up-front production costs 223
  getting attention of traditional publishers 225
  instant delivery 224
  larger margins 223
  powerful marketing tool 224
  speed to market 222–223
e-books, disadvantages of 225
  reputation as poor cousin of physical book 226
Edison, Thomas 57
editing 126–138. *See also* copy-editing
  avoiding language that dates the book 131
  considering additional material for book 127–128

editing ruthlessly 132–133
keeping book's objective clear 131
others' material, importance of acknowledging 128–130
professional editing and proofreading, importance of 135–138
putting book aside to rest 132
reading out loud for better editing 126–127
receiving constructive feedback 133–135
unnecessary words, removing 133
Elance.com 160, 161
electronic books. *See* e-books
electronic rights 183
e-publishing, changing the face of publishing 221
e-reader formats
  AZW 221
  ePub 221
  Mobi 221
e-readers
  iPad 4, 220
  iPad versus Kindle 220
  Kindle 4, 220
  Kobo 4, 220
  Nook 4, 220
  Sony Reader 4, 220
expert, positioning yourself as.
    See book, writing and having one: establishing you as expert

F
Facebook 6, 46, 48, 131, 140
features-versus-benefits argument 86
fees, charging higher 5, 41–44
film rights 182
Financial Times Group 188

G
Gates, Bill 18
ghostwriter 144, 145

description of 147–149
finding one 161–163
hiring, cost of 159–161
how it works 149–151
who suited to 159
ghostwriter hiring, advantages of
152–157
assessment and comprehension check
155–156
assisting with content 153
contacts in publishing 157
contract suggestions 164–165
determining book structure 152
leveraging time and effort 154–155
managing expectations 164
speed 154
working relationship 163–164
ghostwriter hiring, disadvantages of
157–159
cost 157–158
feeling removed from your book
158–159
Gladwell, Malcolm 73, 102
global marketplace, competing in 64,
243
global recognition 54
Godin, Seth 26, 102, 224–226
Guru.com 160, 161

H

hook, having a 59–60

I

iBookstore 220, 223
ideal client 80–81, 83, 87
Ideavirus 224, 226
I.D. System™ 46–47, 76
information, revealing too much.
See secrets, giving away
Ingram 223
Instinctive Drive (I.D.) 131. See I.D.
System™

intellectual property (IP) 57
protecting your 57–61
iPad. See e-readers: iPad
ISBN (International Standard Book
Number) 177, 182, 202
iTunes 220, 223

J

The Jenkins Group survey 3
Johnson, Dr Spencer 101
John Wiley & Sons. See publishers: John
Wiley & Sons
Jud, Brian 233
Jung, Carl 12

K

Kindle. See e-readers: Kindle
King, Stephen 191, 226
Kiyosaki, Robert 52, 253
Kobo. See e-readers: Kobo

L

leads, book generating more 5, 32–34
legacy book, creating your 102, 103,
108
Le Prince, Augustin 57
Levitt, Steven D. 102
Lightening Source Incorporated (LSI)
208–209
loyalty building 38

M

marketing. See also book, writing and
having one; See also book writing process, marketing perspective
in economic downturn 67–68
traditional marketing 66–67
marketing tool. See book, writing and
having one
Matthew, Patrick 58
Meanwell, Michael 225

Microsoft 13, 15, 18, 66, 99
Microsoft PC 18
mind map. *See* book writing process:
    mind map, creating:
Mitchell, Margaret 191
motion picture camera 57

N

niche groups, focusing on 79
Nook. *See* e-readers: Nook

O

online freelance sites 161
Orwell, George 115, 116

P

Pareto principle 64, 244
Pavlov's bell 21
Pavlov's dogs 21
Pepsi 22
perception, importance of 66
Pink, Daniel 102
planning of book. *See* book writing
    process: planning of book
print-on-demand (POD)
  choosing your publishing name 234
  description of 207–209
  POD is not vanity publishing 214
  uploading files 210
  who best suited to 213
print-on-demand (POD), advantages of
    209–211
  access to sales channels 211
  environmentally friendly 211
  flexibility to update and personalise
    210–211
  lower up-front costs 209
  quality indistinguishable from tradi-
    tional publishing 211
  receiving books quickly 211
print-on-demand (POD), disadvantages
    of 212–213

lower profit margins 212
possible restricting contracts 212
reputation question marks 213
products and services, offering addi-
    tional 45–49
profile, book lifting your 32
psychometric profiling tool. *See* I.D.
    System™
publishers
  HarperCollins 187
  Harvard Business Review Press 188
  Holtzbrinck Publishing Holdings 188
  John Wiley & Sons 8, 53, 187, 253
  McGraw-Hill 187
  Pearson 188
  Pearson Education 188
  Penguin 188
  Random House 187
  Scholastic 188
  Simon & Schuster 188
  Time Warner 188
publishing
  e-publishing. *See* e-books
  print-on-demand (POD). *See* print-
    on-demand (POD)
  self-publishing. *See* self-publishing
  traditional publishing. *See* traditional
    publishing
publishing strategy, selecting the appro-
    priate 231–235

Q

Qualman, Eric 66
quotes
  Ash, Mary Kay 241
  Ayres, Elizabeth 112
  Bell, Chip 27
  Bettger, Frank 47
  Brande, Dorothea 143
  Carlyle, Thomas 8
  Chambers, Oswald 231
  Cicero 51
  Colton, Charles Caleb 173

Confucius 76
Darrow, Clarence 18
Disraeli, Benjamin 45
Duell, Charles H. 129
Ecclesiastes 116
Faulkner, William 132
Ford, Henry 20
Godin, Seth 26
Goethe 109
Harding, Ford 33, 37
Hill, Terry H. 65
Jowett, Benjamin 41
Kranz, Jonathon 51
LeBoeuf, Michael 219
Lessing, Doris 191
Levinson, Jay 17
Lincoln, Abraham 73
Marx, Groucho 3
Milne, A. A. 73
Orwell, George 115
Poynter, Dan 197
Proust, Marcel 147
Raleigh, Sir Walter 63
Satterfield, Mark 38
Schopenhauer, Arthur 244
Schwab, Charles M. 31
Smith, Sydney 109
Socrates 53
Strunk Jr., William 133
Urichuck, Bob 33, 42
Vamos, John 35
Virgil 15
Vonnegut, Kurt 110
Weiss, Alan 41, 51
Wheeler, Bill 125
Zinsser, William 116, 125

R

RainToday.com and Wellesley Hills
    Group survey and report 4, 22,
    25, 27, 31, 33, 41, 51, 128, 143,
    158, 159
Redfield, James 213

return on investment, writing a book
    33
revenue streams, creating additional
    45–49
Rowling, J. K. 74, 191
royalty income 26–27, 183–185

S

SalesDogs 52, 94, 253
secrets, giving away 103–104
self-publishing
    not looking self-published 176
    recent improvements 197
    versus traditionally published book.
        See traditional publishing: versus
        self-published book
    who best suited to 203–204
self-publishing, advantages of 198–202
    future business development opportu-
        nities 201–202
    greater revenue 201
    having full control of book 198–201
self-publishing, disadvantages of
    202–203
    organising everything 202
    paying up-front 202–203
    responsibility for sales 203
Singer, Blair 52, 94, 253
slush pile. See traditional publishing:
        slush pile
social media
    Facebook 6
    Twitter 6
Sony Reader. See e-readers: Sony Reader
speaking engagements and seminars
    51–53
    generating more 4
structure of book, importance of.
        See book writing process: struc-
        ture, importance of
surveys and reports. See The Times
        report on book sales; See The
        Jenkins Group survey; See Rain-

Today.com and Wellesley Hills Group survey and report

T

Taleb, Nassim Nicholas 53
testimonials, importance of 36–37
theory of evolution 58
The Times report on book sales 27
thought leader, positioning yourself as 60
title or working title. *See* book writing process: title or working title
trade paperback book format. *See* book formats: B-format
traditional publishing
  book rejections 191
  chances of publishing unsolicited manuscript 173–174, 189
  changes to the industry 192
  little genuine advantage for majority of authors 191
  no formula for bestseller. *See* bestseller, no formula for:
  partnership arrangements 192
  publisher hierarchy 187–189
  publishing proposal, preparing 189–193
  securing a contract 187–193
  slush pile 173, 190
  tier one publishers 187–188
  versus self-published book 175
  who best suited to 185–186
  who is of interest to them 186–187
traditional publishing, advantages of 174–179
  credibility 174–177
  marketing 179
  production expertise 177–178
traditional publishing, disadvantages of 180–185
  difficulty getting published 180
  long lead times 181–182
  losing control of your book 182–183

poor financial rewards 183–185
tricks of the trade, giving away. *See* secrets, giving away
Twitter 6, 46

U

Unique Selling Proposition (USP). *See* book writing process, marketing perspective: Unique Selling Proposition (USP), knowing your
US Trade book format. *See* book formats: Demy

V

value, measures of 6–7
vanity publishing 214–215

W

Wallace, Alfred Russel 58
Wellesley Hills Group. *See* RainToday. com and Wellesley Hills Group survey and report
Word Architect 234
wordarchitect.com 161, 192, 244, 254
writing 110–119
  appropriate voice and style, selecting 112–113
  as you speak 115–117
  audio recording thoughts 119
  clear, precise language, using 115–116
  dictating the book 120
  information, keeping at hand 118
  jargon, avoiding 115
  length of sentences and paragraphs, varying 117
  making it easy to read 117
  notebook, keeping of 119
  personality, showing your 112–113
  reading to improve writing 120
  subjective nature of 110–111
  text, breaking up of 117

using examples, research and quotations 114
without judgement 118–119

About The Author

Karen McCreadie is a prolific and flexible writer capable of taking complex information and making it accessible to a wider audience. She started her career in marketing after graduating university with a business degree. In 1997 she moved to Sydney, Australia, where she continued her career in marketing before taking the plunge as a self-employed writer three years later. Karen now ghostwrites non-fiction business and personal development titles for a niche market and has successfully worked with CEOs, multi-millionaire business owners, entrepreneurs, international speakers, health professionals and professional services practitioners.

Her first book, *SalesDogs* by Blair Singer, is now an international bestseller and part of Robert Kiyosaki's *Rich Dad's Advisors* series. Since then Karen has written, co-authored, authored and ghostwritten over 35 books on topics as diverse as sales, wealth creation, property development, business coaching, change management, sports psychology and personal development. Karen's business background and marketing expertise creates a powerful combination, especially when helping others to write a book for marketing and business development purposes. Working alongside an expert, Karen can write in a broad range of non-fiction areas.

As well as being a ghostwriter, Karen is also an author in her own right. She has been commissioned to write books a number of times by top publisher John Wiley & Sons – including a TV tie-in for the Australian TV show *Auction Squad*, and a couple of business biographies of well-known Australian entrepreneurs. She has also been commissioned by Infinite Ideas, a UK publisher, to write modern interpretations of classic books, *The Art of War, Think and Grow Rich, The Richest Man in Babylon, The*

Wealth of Nations, How I Raised Myself from Failure to Success in Selling and *Secret of the Ages.* These books, which were published under the *Infinite Success* series, identified 52 of the most important points raised in each of the original books. These points were then individually brought up to date through a modern day case study or the introduction of new research or scientific understanding in order to emphasise the continued relevance of these classic books.

For an up-to-date bibliography of the books Karen has been involved in visit www.wordarchitect.com.